SARTREAN ETHICS

A DEFENSE OF JEAN-PAUL SARTRE AS A MORAL PHILOSOPHER

BEN WOOD JOHNSON

EDUKA ⚥ SOLUTIONS

SARTREAN ETHICS

A Defense of Jean-Paul Sartre as a Moral Philosopher

Ben Wood Johnson

Edited by

Ben Wood Johnson

Eduka Solutions/Tesko Publishing
MIDDLETOWN, PENNSYLVANIA, USA

Copyright © 2021 by Tesko Publishing/Eduka Solutions.

Middletown, Pennsylvania 17057.

Copyright © 2016 by Ben Wood Johnson. All rights reserved.

No part of this publication may be reproduced, distributed, or transmitted in any form or by any means, including photocopying, recording, or other electronic or mechanical methods, or by any information storage and retrieval system without the prior written permission of the publisher, except in the case of very brief quotations embodied in critical reviews and certain other noncommercial uses permitted by copyright law.

The information illustrated in this book was compiled for a school project. The analysis is based on class notes and other materials.

Ben Wood, Johnson
    Sartrean Ethics: A Defense of Jean-Paul Sartre as a Moral Philosopher/
    Ben Wood Johnson. 1975—
    This text includes bibliographical references and index.

This book was first published in September 2016

ISBN-13: 978-0-9979028-0-8 (pbk.)
ISBN-10: 0-997902-80-9

Tesko Publishing/Eduka Solutions

330 W. Main St. #214
Middletown, PA 17057, USA

Official website address: www.teskopublishing.com

Printed in the United States of America

This book was designed by Xaon Prime Studios

Cover illustration by Wood Oliver

To my mother (Mama)
For guiding my steps, even from beyond the grave.

TABLE OF CONTENTS

PREFACE XIII

INTRODUCTION 1
    Book Structure 3

1. PUBLICATIONS ABOUT ETHICS 7
    The Crux of the Debate 10
    Analysis and Challenges 13
    Conducting a Formal Inquiry 14

2. ASSESSING UNFAIR CRITICISMS 19
    Treading With Caution 21
    Taking Criticisms Seriously 24
    The Failed Promise 25
    The Importance of Criticisms 28

3. ASSESSING SARTRE'S TRUE INTENT 35
    Arlette Elkaïm-Sartre Clarifies 37
    Outlining My Goals 40
    Refuting the Arguments 41

TABLE OF CONTENTS

 Inconsistent Criticisms 42
 Denying Sartrean Ethics 45
 Pseudo-Moral Philosopher 47

4. EXAMINING SARTREAN ETHICS *53*

 Searching for a Method 56
 Limits 58
 A Simplistic Approach 60
 Examining Posthumous Works 61
 Lack of Theoretical Scheme 63
 Refuting Sartrean Ethics 65

5. A HOUSEHOLD NAME *71*

 Examining Diverging Positions 73
 Points of Conflict 75
  The Publication Argument *76*
  Works Published Versus Works Produced *78*
  The Substance Argument *79*
  The Theoretical Argument *80*
 The Holistic Argument 83

6. SARTRE'S MAJOR WORKS *89*

 Important Works About Ethics 91
 Unpublished Materials 95
 Examining the Notebooks 98
  Being and Non-Being *99*

7. THE SCOPE OF SARTREAN ETHICS *105*

 The Individual and the Community 107
 Denying Sartrean Ethics 109
 Authentic Individual and Ethics 111

8. UNDERSTANDING SARTREAN ETHICS *117*

 A Long Search for Identity 119
 The Link Between Freedom and Ethics 121

Perception of "The Other" 122
The Ontological Experience 123

9. A NEED TO GIVE SARTRE CREDIT *127*

Placing Sartrean Ethics 130
Describing Sartrean Ethics.. 131
The Elusive Sartrean Ethics 134

10. A COMMONSENSE APPROACH.. *141*

Historical Factors 142
Early Ethics and Freedom... 143
Intentional Acts Versus Being.. 145
An Abstract Ethics.. 146
Examining the Role of Consciousness... 147
Assessing the Essence of Sartrean Ethics..................................... 148

11. THE EFFECTS OF SOCIETY *153*

Freedom and Society 154
Society Affects Ethics... 155
Ethical Normative 156
Mutual Recognition 156
Morality and Lack 157

12. A CALL FOR A BETTER APPROACH... *163*

Mistaken Viewpoints.. 164
A Positive Scrutiny of Sartrean Ethics... 165
Sartrean Ethics and Human Existence 166
Carrying Out My Goals 167

FINAL WORDS *173*

Wrapping-Up the Debate... 174
The Foundation of This Book 175

APPENDICES... *179*

BIBLIOGRAPHY *189*

TABLE OF CONTENTS

> Recommended Readings 191
> ACKNOWLEDGMENTS 199
> INDEX.. 201
> ABOUT THE AUTHOR.. 213
> OTHER WORKS 215

Table Of Figures

Figure 5. 1: Approaches to Sartrean Ethics 77
Figure 6. 1: Posthumously Released Works 96
Figure 10. 1: Categories of Sartrean Ethics 144

Appendices

Appendix A: Selected Books 181
Appendix B: Selected Magazines 183
Appendix C: Selected Academic Journals 185
Appendix D: Selected Newspapers 187

Table Of Figures And Appendices

Preface

You would probably share the view, which purports that there is no dearth of information about Jean-Paul Sartre. He is among the most studied thinkers in human history. The literature is filled with writings that are dedicated to analyzing Sartre and his theories about human ontology, even though many of such publications can be critical and unforgiving toward Sartre and his works.

Many years ago, I attended a course about Jean-Paul Sartre.[1] As a final project, I had to write an essay that examines the extent of Sartrean ethics. I reviewed several publications about Sartre. I examined views that praised the Sartrean approach to moral philosophy. I reviewed writings that criticized his contribution to the discipline. A few scholarly works caught my attention.

The more I learned about Sartre, the more I realized that criticisms against him [or against his works] can be misplaced. I noticed that critics could be fierce toward Sartre. The common

---

[1] I was a graduate student at Villanova University. I was completing my works for a degree in Political Science.

argument is that Sartre played little or no role in moral philosophy. I do not share such a viewpoint. In the present context, I hope to refute this understanding as much as I can. There is enough evidence to suggest that Sartre played a substantial role in the ethical discipline.

While compiling the final project, I consulted blogs, books, magazines, papers, and scholarly articles about Sartre. Although many analysts examined Sartre's overall achievements in literature, others were critical of the man, including his life choices and his personality. Other works even questioned Sartre's moral character.[2]

I found the literature overly critical of Jean-Paul Sartre. I saw that most contentions against the man centered on his approach to ethics. I could not make sense of criticisms against Sartre. I decided to compile a book, which would help clarify the debate.

After examining the arguments that are often levied against Sartre, I found them derisory. They do not hold up under scrutiny. They do not provide enough insights, which could justify the current trends against the relevance of Sartrean ethics. I have a different outlook regarding that ethics. I wanted to interject that approach in the debate. Throughout this work, I echo that perspective as compellingly as possible.

This text is a way to change the conversation. It is designed to be both informative and intellectually entertaining. The book features an array of viewpoints that could be considered provocative by many readers. The views expressed here could also be considered captivating by others.

Despite potential negative interpretations of my objects in compiling this work, this paperback was designed to be reader friendly. My arguments are intended to engage the reader

---

[2] See the book *Sartre Lives On* to learn more about criticisms. You may also see *Jean-Paul Sartre and Morality: A Legacy Under Attack* to find out how criticisms against Jean-Paul Sartre can be misplaced.

intellectually. An alternative goal is to promote a smooth reading experience.

Those who are familiar with Sartrean philosophy will get a good sense of the views I echo here. Those who have little or no familiarity with the Sartrean approach to moral philosophy will learn about a side of Jean-Paul Sartre, which is seldom explored in positive terms in the literature. They will uncover the way many people sought to tarnish the Sartrean literary legacy.

Completing this book was daunting. The goal was to satisfy the reader's curiosity about Sartre. I sought to carry out that aim in the most simplistic method. Another goal was to refute criticisms against Sartre.

I did not want to compile a complicated book. I did not want this work to be too academic; I did not want it to be unsophisticated to a point of having no real clout in the literature. The same, I did not want to compile a book that repeats popular arguments against Sartre. I offer a different approach in the debate. This was not easy, considering that English is not my native tongue.

I wanted to find the right tone to express my concerns. I wanted to outline my views in an acceptable, but also a collegial, manner. I wanted to examine criticisms against Sartrean ethics in the most vivid passion. I sought to carry my thoughts with an innocuous parole. I think I found the right format to make this text captivating.

Agreed, whether I succeed in my efforts will be up to you (that is, the reader) to decide. Anyway, I hope this work will start a substantive conversation about the senseless nature of assaults against Sartre, which generally characterize the discourse on the issue of Sartrean ethics. I hope that it will help you make sense of the current discourse about Jean-Paul Sartre.

PREFACE

In sum, the views I echo in this book are logical. My arguments are concise. But a warning is worth mentioning before we delve in the manuscript. While my positions are laid out analytically, they are not chronological; they are not devoid of my own idiosyncrasies. I encourage you to consider these limits as you make your way through the manuscript.

Good Reading!
Ben Wood Johnson, Ph.D.
January 2021

Updated April 2021

INTRODUCTION

Jean-Paul Sartre is under attack. This claim is not hysteria. It is not an exaggeration. It is not hyperbole.

The Sartrean literary legacy in moral philosophy is under siege. I offer a defense of this philosopher. But that defense, I must point out, does not encompass every constituent of the Sartrean literary repertoire. That defense, to be clear, is narrower; it focuses on ethics.[3]

I examine how Jean-Paul Sartre was able to link morality with human freedom. This work, to reiterate, is about the Sartrean approach to moral philosophy.[4] The hope is to help settle the ideas, which Sartre often voiced in the domain.

I examine views expressed by prominent scholars, including, but not limited to, David Pellauer, Ji Ruman, Thomas Flynn, Thomas Anderson, Robert Stone, Elizabeth Bowman, Ronald Aronson, Adrian Van Den Hoven, Richard Bernstein, David

---

[3] I am referring to the Sartrean approach to human morality.

[4] I use the term Sartrean ethics to describe the nature of the writings, which Sartre produced in this discipline.

Introduction

Detmer, and Heter Storm. The goal is to question arguments, which dominate the literature.

Although this work is subtitled a *defense of Jean-Paul Sartre as a Moral Philosopher*, it is not a combative stance on Sartre's behalf. I tried to lay out my arguments as compellingly as possible. Keep in mind that examining Sartrean ethics can be a complex undertaken.

Sartre was a controversial thinker. But not much is known about him. This work questions the relevance of popular assumptions about Sartre and his literary accomplishments. Many of the views that pervade the literature are inaccurate. These criticisms were designed to smear Jean-Paul Sartre.

The present work is not perfect. It might invite speculations about Sartre. But I hope to examine the issues objectively. By contrast, I do not want to incite unnecessary distractions in the debate.

Jean-Paul Sartre died many years ago (April 1980). Some observers might say that his literary legacy is well established. His fame is solidified in popular culture. But it would not be exaggerated to point out that the Sartrean legacy is constantly under attack. It is not clear how long the Sartrean imprint in modern literature will last. Hence, there is a need to defend the Sartrean heritage tooth and nails. In this book, I propose to do just that.

My point is that Sartre is still a relevant thinker in contemporary literature. Sartrean philosophy still has an intellectual merit. There is no need to undermine Sartre; there is no need to undermine his intellectual legacy.

Despite the previous assertion, I recognize that the philosophy, which Jean-Paul Sartre pioneered, is not easy to digest. His works are not easy to discern. Perhaps this is the roots of criticisms against the man; perhaps this is the reason critics often lash out against his works as well. Nonetheless, examining Sartre is a worthy academic effort. Sartrean ethics is an important topic. Bear in mind that apart from ethics, my analysis includes Sartre's popular works about human ontology, notably *existentialism*.

BOOK STRUCTURE

This work was originally a voluptuous manuscript. After its initial publication, I decided to republish a streamlined version of the document. Out of that process came three distinct books. They include the present text, *Jean-Paul Sartre and Morality (A Legacy Under Attack)* and *Sartre Lives On*. Each compilation is available as separate tomes.

The present volume is divided in twelve chapters. It contains a concluding part, which includes remarks and other notes. The manuscript includes other materials and the sources cited. The final section of the text includes a bibliography and a summary of my major arguments.

The book features several works, which examine Jean-Paul Sartre himself as well as his major philosophical approaches. The document includes appendices and other references. It outlines Sartre's literary imprint in human history.

The arguments echoed throughout this work are not the results of an exhaustive empirical investigation. Here, nonetheless, I elaborate on Sartre's major philosophical accomplishments, notably his ideas about human ontology. The text outline criticisms (both productive and destructive remarks) against [or in favor of] Sartrean ethics. The book further echoes the views, which had been recorded by three prominent scholars. These famed commentators include Thomas C. Anderson, Robert V. Stone, and Elizabeth A. Bowman. Keep in mind that the text itself is not based only on the treaties listed by the noted scholars. It includes

Introduction

viewpoints echoed by other commentators. Let us delve deeper in the manuscript.

Chapter One

The Great Debate

This chapter assesses the nub of Sartre's contribution to literature. The focus here is on his views about morality. The chapter examines Sartre's recent publications in the field; it explores the crux of the debate. The chapter elaborates on the origin of the conversation against the Sartrean approach to moral philosophy. It hinges on the methods I used to evaluate the nature of Jean-Paul Sartre's contribution to ethics. It explores the degree to which we should take criticisms seriously.

CHAPTER

1

PUBLICATIONS ABOUT ETHICS

Jean-Paul Sartre was not new to ethical writings. He produced several materials about ethics, including a book titled *Notebooks for an Ethics*. Sartre compiled this work between 1947 and 1948. Sartre produced an array of other literary items, which, by my understanding alone, are irrefutably suitable for ethics. Such materials include, but are not limited to, published interviews, speeches, and essays. These papers were compiled between the mid-1960s and the mid-1970s.[1]

A limited number of these items had been published during Sartre's lifetime. The notebooks, for instance, were originally published in 1983 by his adoptive daughter (Arlette Elkaïm-Sartre).² These texts had been released nearly three years after Sartre died.³

The other documents that Sartre produced on the subject had been uncovered in the 1990s. For many observers, this is proof that Sartre was not a prolific writer in the ethical domain. Sartre could not be considered a moral philosopher, critics say. But I beg to differ.

The few items, which Sartre produced, bewildered observers propose, are short, rambling, and inconclusive. The pervading belief is that Sartre has no literary relevance in the ethical domain. To say it again, I disagree. Here is why.

Sartre has an imprint in the ethical discipline, although most of his texts were published posthumously. Granted, it might be exaggerated to refer to Sartre's posthumous publications, more intentionally the uncovered materials, as a testimony of his contribution to ethics. It might be difficult to make out the instrumentality of the role that Sartre might have played in ethics. It would be equally ill-advised to examine the nature of Sartrean ethics by relying solely on the recently released materials. Nonetheless, it is imperative to have a better read of these lines. This is the best way, I would argue, to get a grasp of the Sartrean approach to moral philosophy.

To decode the extent of Sartrean ethics, it is vital to review the publications that Sartre produced specifically about ethics. It is central to grasp the theoretical foundations of Sartrean ethics. That view must be the result of the ideas, which Sartre explained in his own words, including in items that he compiled about phenomenology. Delineating a clear link between Sartrean philosophy and Sartrean ethics is a good place to start.

The philosophical writings of Jean-Paul Sartre are notoriously convoluted. They are laden with abstract concepts. There is not an exact manner to study the Sartrean model of philosophy. It might be difficult to appreciate the ethical groundwork of the views contained in those manuscripts. Even so, it makes sense to examine the essence of Sartrean ethics through his approach to human ontology, although we could do so only from a shallow perspective.

While I do not explore Sartrean philosophy in depth, I rely on the ideas echoed in many of Sartre's major publications. This is the best way to understand the nature of Sartrean ethics. I carry out that goal by examining what Sartre's major publications, notably the views he expressed in the book titled *Being and Nothingness*, could tell us about the Sartrean ethical model.

The treaties that Sartre published about phenomenology [in this case, his notions about human freedom] are important to help us understand the extent of his intellectual identity in the ethical discipline. My analysis contains titles, which Sartre published himself (that is, while alive) and postmortem releases (that is, materials published after his death). To be specific, this book resulted from works, which Sartre produced himself, including writings published on his behalf (by Elkaïm-Sartre) and works published about Sartre (by well-known Sartrean scholars or other critics). In any case, this work echoes an all-inclusive approach in the debate.

Before we delve further in the manuscript, let us examine the crux of the issues. Let us scrutinize the marrow of criticisms. Let us explore the nature of the current discourse, which generally fustigates Sartre's literary works about moral philosophy.

Chapter 1: Publications About Ethics

The Crux of the Debate

Many commentators argue that it would be premature to rely only on the posthumously released materials to treat Sartre as a moral philosopher. Even if we could set up the boundaries of Sartre's contribution to the field, they say, it might still be difficult, if not impossible, to find out the extent of his moral thoughts. I disagree with that understanding. Jean-Paul Sartre would probably share my position. Here is why…

Sartre always considered himself a moral philosopher. He never missed the opportunity to restate his intellectual identity in the ethical discipline. During an interview Sartre gave in 1978, he stated that he never stopped being a moral philosopher.[4]

Throughout his career, Sartre worked continuously to develop an approach to ethics, which is worthy of his intellectual talents. Therefore, depriving Sartre of the title of a moral philosopher would be wrong. It would be unethical, to say the least.

Another point of dissent often resounded in the literature is that Sartrean ethics lacks a clear intellectual framework. Such an ethics is devoid of a clear analytical structure. Critics even contended that there is no Sartrean ethics.

An important nuance is worth stressing in the debate. Indeed, several parts of Sartre's theses about ethics lack a clear structure. This is not surprising, considering that it is well documented that Sartre's posthumous texts are fragmented. Even his daughter (Elkaïm-Sartre) recognized that indiscriminate features of the notes that her father produced lack a clear structure. In the introductory section of the book titled « *Cahiers pour une morale,* » she addressed this drawback head-on. She writes:

> « Ces 'Notes', bien qu'écrites au courant de la plume et non relues, sont un peu plus que des notes ; elles ont un fil et sont souvent plus

qu'à demi rédigées. Mais elles n'ont pas de structure : l'index, qui ne se prétend pas exhaustif, a pour but de compenser un peu cette absence, en suggérant quelques contours ».

Translation:

> "These 'Notes,' even though they are handwritten and have not been reviewed, are a little more than just notes; they have a pattern and are often semi developed. They do not have any structure: the index, which is not exhaustive, seems to compensate that lack of structure and suggests some outlines."

As noted in *Cahiers pour une morale*, (1983, p. 8).

The difference in the debate here is that the lack of structure, which Elkaïm-Sartre evoked in her assessment, does not sync with the argumentative structure, which observers are concerned about. Elkaïm-Sartre's viewpoint differs from the analysis commentators have repeatedly pointed out. The lack of structure previously quoted stand for a stylistic inconsistency within the essays that Sartre produced. This could be relegated to the flow of the arguments or the format of the notes themselves, rather than the cogency of their contents.

Critics, on the other hand, seem more interested in sketching out the argumentative structure of the materials Sartre compiled. They appear more concerned about the convincingness of the argument Sartre related in his writings. They are prone to refute his role in ethics solely on that understanding. But this is a misguided way of gauging Sartre's philosophy, chiefly when it comes to the role, which Sartre seemingly played in ethics.

Critics argue that what is understood about Sartre's approach to morality is inadequate to concede that his posthumous collection forms the foundation of his ethics. Critics echo that even Sartre seldom claimed that he developed a strong instrumentation to understand the extent of human morality. I

Chapter 1: Publications About Ethics

disagree with that view. I explain in chapter 2 that Sartre had a clear sense of his intellectual identity in ethics.

Critics also noted that no one knows what Sartrean ethics is or what such an approach to moral philosophy could be. Any hint of that ethics, commentators are convinced, is trivial. Others argued that such an ethics, regardless of its form or structure, must be considered non-existent.

Robert Stone and Elizabeth Bowman note that it is likely that the views Sartre developed in his works about human morality might be called the missing center of Sartre's project as a philosopher. They further point out that Sartre seemed content with these writings.[5] I echo a similar sentiment in this book.

From this point of departure, the task I propose here might seem impossible. But I will labor to reference the relevant pieces of literature, which would allow a better understanding of the issues. This collection proposes a different perspective about the views that are often recounted in the literature. The challenge is to provide enough evidence to support my arguments.

The approach I have taken in this work is neither argumentative nor persuasive. The objective is to put forth a new lens through which to examine the issues. To put it in a different term, the object of this work is to interject a neutral stream in the present literary discussion about Sartrean ethics.

This text projects a novel scheme to examine Sartrean ethics. But the ideas featured here are not paralleled from the types of arguments that are often resounded in the literature. The tone of my arguments is supposed to be conciliatory and even allegorical.

Analysis and Challenges

Many scholars tried to show that Sartre had no role in moral philosophy. They did not even give him the presumption of success in the discipline. The literature is filled with writings, which categorically refute the possibility that Sartre might have played any role in ethics. After I reviewed a few of these publications, I came up with a different perspective. I have a different understanding of Sartre's true literary valor in the ethical domain.

I examined whether popular positions against Sartre reflect his true literary worth. I examined the debate, which affirms or rejects the utility of the essays, which Sartre produced about ethics. I assessed the writings that examined the written materials recently minted on Sartre's behalf. Such literary works include unpublished lectures and unreleased manuscripts.

Despite the rise of discussions debasing Sartrean ethics, I am unmoved by many of these criticisms. I am not sure that Sartre is a failure in moral philosophy. As a minimum, this is not that way simply because the treaties, which Sartre produced, are fragmented or uncompleted. I am unconvinced that Sartre has no relevance in ethical writings. Let me elaborate further on that understanding.

I could point out a few texts, which had been authored by several scholars. This collection of viewpoints discuss how Sartre contributed to ethics. The travail logged by Thomas Anderson, Robert Stone, and Elizabeth Bowman reinforced my belief that Sartre has a relevant role in moral philosophy. After examining the noted narratives, it became clear to me that, in all certainty, a genuine Sartrean ethics exists.

I would admit that Sartrean ethics is embryonic. It is that way in many respects. That ethics is fragmented. But critics are inclined to refute that ethics on the premise that Sartre's posthumous texts are incomplete. I do not share that view.

A circular argument is worth pointing out in the debate. First, critics classify Sartre's writings about moral philosophy as incomplete. Then, they judge them insignificant for intellectual consumptions precisely because they are labeled incomplete.

While I agree that most of Sartre's materials are fragmentary, I do not think this fact is enough to devalue them. It is unclear whether critics reject Sartre's literary accomplishments because they are unsuitable for ethical writings or whether it is because such works come from Sartre. I am not sure of the relevance of criticisms against Sartrean ethics.

It is true that the number of publications, which Sartre produced about ethics, is relatively small, at least in comparison to the body of materials that he published in other areas, namely in phenomenology. It could be difficult to argue in favor of Sartre in the ethical discipline. All the same, it could be challenging to take seriously views that support the notion that Sartre has little or no standing in moral philosophy.

Conducting a Formal Inquiry

It is not right to refute the value of Sartre's written works only by referencing the scope of his arguments. It makes little sense to rebuke Sartrean ethics on the publication ground alone. The debate does not have to center on whether Sartre was prolific in ethics. Points of dispute would have a more impact if they relied on the quality of the written materials, which Sartre produced in the domain.

The three scholars mentioned earlier (in this case, Anderson, Stone, and Bowman) proved that Sartre's literary imprints, including writings published while alive and other posthumously released materials, contain a true ethics. Of course, whether that ethics encompasses a strong theoretical foundation is a different question, which we could examine separately or we could do so within a different context. To reiterate, such an inquiry is not my aim in the present work.

Let me point out that completing this book was challenging. The biggest obstacle, I must say, is that I could not locate neutral viewpoints on the matter. Most often, the positions echoed in the literature are uniformed against Sartre. Few scholarly publications support Sartre's positions about ethics. For the most part, it is a complete rebuke. Nonetheless, there are positive remarks about Sartrean ethics.

As noted earlier, there are dissenting approaches in the debate disputing arguments against the scope of Sartrean ethics. But these views, I must admit, are in the minority. Still, they exist. Unlike the majority of works that examine Sartre and his role in ethics, some scholars in the field hold a different viewpoint about the role Sartre played in constructing his ethics.

There is not much division in the literature. Still, I wanted to explore the issues deeper. Considering my experience while conducting the research for the final project in Dr. Busch's course, I anticipated a difficult research experience, for I could not conceive finding works that present a balanced view about Sartrean ethics. I assumed that conducting a formal inquiry about the subject would be overburdened and, frankly, unnecessary. The prospect of collecting reliable data about Sartrean appeared unrealistic. I concluded that any efforts to locate unbiassed information about Sartre via a formal inquiry would be in futility.

Because of the scarcity of cogent viewpoints, it became clear to me that it would be difficult to conduct a full-blown study about Sartrean ethics. I opted for a simplistic approach. Therefore, this work is a light defense of Jean-Paul Sartre in the ethical discipline. Chapter 3 discusses the technique I used in detail.

Chapter Notes

[1] Anderson, *Sartre's Two Ethics*, 2.

[2] In 1964, Sartre adopted Arlette Elkaïm. She was 29 years old. At the time, she was studying philosophy.

[3] Sartre died in 1980 in France.

[4] Stone and Bowman, "Sartre's Morality and History: A First Look at the Notes for the Unpublished 1965 Cornell Lectures," 56. (Interview with Sicard, 14)

[5] Ibid.

Chapter Two

Relevance of Criticisms

This chapter relates how criticisms against Jean-Paul Sartre are unfair. It examines the potential reasons, which led Sartre to promise to dedicate a future work to ethics. The chapter assesses the degree to which criticisms against Sartrean ethics are warranted or even intellectually relevant. It discusses whether such debasing evaluations of the works Sartre produced about ethics are worthy of attention. Here as well, I pose my central argument as clearly as possible.

CHAPTER

2

Assessing Unfair Criticisms

When it comes to moral philosophy, Jean-Paul Sartre published fewer works—while alive—that were manifestly tailored for ethics. But that fact alone is not enough to classify him as an unimportant thinker in the field. This is so even though he produced a plethora of other writings, which are inextricably related to ethics. Critics contend the opposite.

I would argue that criticisms are unfair. In my view, there is more to uncover about Sartre's moral thoughts than relegating his works as incomplete. There is more to the issues than a mere analysis of his posthumous releases. Nevertheless, criticisms that emanated from a meager examination of such essays are shallow; they lack a clear intellectual frame of reference.

The Sartrean approach to ethics is more intense than a measly glimpse of the positions Sartre highlighted in his posthumously uncovered works. But understandings about his approach to ethics seldom reflect his other writings. I propose to examine Sartrean ethics by considering his major theory about human existence.

Sartrean ethics is interlaced with human ontology. Every human conduct has ethical ramifications. In the Sartrean world, we could not assess ethics superficially. By way of explanation, it would be difficult to examine ethics parallel to phenomenology.

Examining Sartre's role in ethics needs an all-inclusive approach. Other characteristics of Sartre's literary accomplishments are worthy of scrutiny. Such materials might include, but should not be limited to, the compilations, which he published personally and the literary collections, which Elkaïm-Sartre released posthumously on his behalf. A methodical examination of these writings, I am sure, would offer definitive proofs that Sartre is a moral philosopher in all his glory. This is the case, I would contend, even though it might be hard to argue that Sartre was a meticulous writer in the ethical discipline.

Criticisms that seek to fustigate Sartre are misplaced. Many are unfair. But this is the case so long as they come from a narrow perspective. Many of the criticisms that belittle Sartre or the ones that try to slander him are disjointed. Fewer studies [or scarce analyses] have used a systematic approach to assess the foundations of Sartre's intellectual worth in ethics.[1]

Assessments that rely on less than an all-inclusive scheme provide a one-sided version of the story. Such examinations could not explain the nature of Sartre's true contribution to moral philosophy. There is a need for a novel paradigm in the literature.

What do I mean by a systematic approach? Here, I am referring to a technique that allows a comprehensive examination of Sartrean ethics. Let me explain further, though briefly, what I mean by a *systematic* approach.

TREADING WITH CAUTION

A systematic approach entails a method or a plan, which is crafted specifically to carry out a particular task or a duty.[2] Such a technique would create a process, which would also allow us to examine, though not in depth, the extent of Sartrean ethics.[3] I use a similar approach here.

A methodical review of Sartrean ethics demands an inclusive approach. Doing so would yield a uniformed examination of the issues.[4] If we could not come up with a detailed review of the writings that Jean-Paul Sartre produced about ethics, it might be necessary to tread with caution in our criticisms.

When it comes to examining the crux of Sartrean ethics, a few observers have acted with caution. Commentators recognize that the items, which Sartre produced, are yet to be published. They note that such essays are not available for public scrutiny.[5] They do not want to write off Sartre as a contributor in ethics. Their cynicism stems from the conviction that other writings might surface later. Such publications might be used to solidify Sartre's commitment to moral philosophy.

It is irrefutable that Sartre played a role in the ethical discipline. The foundation of his major ideas in other areas of philosophy implicates ethics. The noteworthy essays, which Sartre is credited to have produced in the field, were released after his death.[6] But that does not annul such materials. This is the crux of the issues.

Chapter 2: Examining Unfair Criticisms

Critics classified most of Sartre's postmortem writings as incongruent and vague. The common belief is that Sartre is a failure in ethics. I disagree with that view. I would argue that there is more to Sartrean ethics than reducing it to a mere subjective assessment of what that ethics is worth. I found it difficult to agree with deductions, which are based only on such a narrow understanding of Sartre's intent in compiling his works about ethics. They seem to miss the point.

Sartre's overall contribution in ethical writings is often overlooked. Should I say that, more often than I could point out, that contribution is simply ignored. There should be more to the debate about Sartre's true role in moral philosophy. There is a need to outline the extent of Sartre's true literary role in ethics. There is a need to establish Sartre's true literary worth in the ethical discipline.

Observers are convinced that they have a mastery of Sartre's real impact on ethics. The view traditionally echoed is that Sartrean ethics is not sophisticated; it is unimpressive; it can be easily disentangled. Others are convinced that Sartre does not have any intellectual relevance in this domain. But there is an incongruity in the debate.

The previous viewpoints contradict the belief that Sartrean ethics is abstract and complicated. One must wonder about the true essence of criticisms. Granted, I am not sure how to assess the issues objectively.

The reach of the Sartrean take about ethics is disputed vigorously. Opponents sought to minimize Sartre's intellectual worth altogether. I am baffled about the reason(s) critics often found it necessary to tie Sartre's overall contribution to philosophy (or literature, for that matter) with his role in ethics.

The correct answer to the previous question eludes me. I am not sure what the true nature of criticism is. But others struggle with the same intrigue. A clear answer about the reason many are so quick to dismiss Sartrean ethics eludes most scholars. Criticisms are out of bound. The debate is out of hand.

In the next few chapters, I outline the reason (I am convinced) Sartrean ethics is often criticized. I examine the motive (I am positive) Jean-Paul Sartre is often the target of senseless rebukes. There is a need to reassess the weight of criticisms.

The literature is not always one-sided. There are helpful criticisms. Many of the writings that offer non-constructive rebukes about the scope of Sartrean ethics outnumber the types of compilations, which offer a useful scrutiny of that ethics. Fewer analysts espouse a neutral stance in the debate. I would describe the present literary conversation as an intellectual onslaught.

Sartre is fustigated from all possible angles. His philosophy is under siege; his literary legacy is under attack, that is, to say the least. His intellectual worth is undermined. For lack of a better explanation, I would say that Sartre is castigated for being Sartre.

The present inquiry offers a succinct review of the debate. But this is so only for the many publications (scholarly or else), which are available about Sartre, including his approach to ethics. My object is to examine the issues succinctly.

It might be difficult to avoid repetitions in the views I express. Here, on the other hand, I offer a substantive analysis. This work explores the poignant arguments that are often echoed against Jean-Paul Sartre, which includes both criticisms and praises. I consider both positive and neutral assessments, which are often echoed in Sartre's favor. I examine views that are often voiced by prominent scholars. Toward the end of the manuscript, the discussions centers on the productive criticisms, which are often levied by the following scholars: Thomas Anderson, Elizabeth Bowman, and Robert Stone.

CHAPTER 2: EXAMINING UNFAIR CRITICISMS

TAKING CRITICISMS SERIOUSLY

It is commonly understood that Sartre could not complete most of his writings. Due to other literary duties, he had to postpone his major ideas about moral philosophy. That fact is undisputable.

Sartre had a deep interest in moral philosophy. He compiled a few texts here and there about ethics. As you would expect, many of his ideas were jotted down as handwritten notes, which Sartre likely compiled in haste.

There is also the possibility that the writings published on Sartre's behalf might not represent his original thoughts. To turn the notes [or the manuscripts], which Sartre produced into a book, someone else would have to review them. If not, his ideas would have to be edited or even rearranged by someone other than Sartre. But this plausibility is not the subject of the present defense.

The essays credited to Jean-Paul Sartre might not be as genuine as one might expect. This likelihood should incite more questions about the authenticity of his contribution in ethics. Most observers do not seem too concerned about that.

I am not sure of the reason that there is less interest in discovering the authenticity of the publications released on Sartre's behalf. In this instance, I am referring to items published posthumously. I do not understand the reason commentators seem more interested in refuting Jean-Paul Sartre by pointing out that he did not follow through with his promise to complete his project about ethics.

Before Sartre concluded his views in *"Being and Nothingness,"* he made a promise to dedicate a future work to ethics. But Sartre did not do so during his lifetime. There are questions about the reason Sartre did not honor this promise. One could say that such a question is already settled. Let us explore Sartre's promise a little closer to make sense of the crux of the issues that it creates.

THE FAILED PROMISE

In trying to understand whether the being exerts any control over the self, notably when it comes to freedom, Sartre pondered on several questions. He also noted that these questions could be best discovered on the ethical plane. In *Being and Nothingness*, he writes:

"Existential psychoanalysis is going to reveal to man the real goal of his pursuit, which is being as a synthetic fusion of the in-itself with the for-itself; existential psychoanalysis is going to acquaint man with his passion."[7]

Sartre sought to prove a clear link between ontology and morality. In the same publication, he writes:

"But ontology and existential psychoanalysis (or the spontaneous and empirical application which men have always made of these disciplines) must reveal to the moral agent that he is the being by whom values exist. It is then that his freedom will become conscious of itself and will reveal itself in anguish as the unique source of value and the nothingness by which the world exists."[8]

Sartre suggests that the being must build the foundation of his freedom. But that construction is only possible if the being could make out the values, which make him a whole. The being must grasp that he alone has the power to be free. The being must also understand that he must first become aware of that possible reality.

Sartre was not certain whether the being would be able to settle the moral agent that would make his freedom possible. Sartre was not sure whether freedom would incite that moral agent before the being could become aware of that reality. Sartre asked several questions, which he recognized that he could not answer on the ontological plane alone. In *Being and Nothingness* (pp. 797-798), he writes:

> *"What will become of freedom if it turns its back upon this value? Will freedom carry this value along with it whatever it does and even in its very turning back upon the in-itself-for-itself? Will freedom be reapprehended from behind by the value, which it wishes to contemplate? Or will freedom, by the very fact that it apprehends itself as a freedom in relation to itself, be able to put an end to the reign of this value? In particular is it possible for freedom to take itself for a value as the source of all value, or must it necessarily be defined in relation to a transcendent value which haunts it? And in case it could will itself as its own possible and its determining value, what would this mean?"*

Sartre tried to prove [eloquently, I would say] a clear outline or the lack of that between freedom and morality. Sartre also recognized that his incapacity to dissociate freedom with human morality, for example via that moral agent, which is the being itself/himself, it would be nearly impossible. Put differently, Sartre seemed unsure about the role of morality onto the individual. In *Being and Nothingness* (p. 798), Sartre further writes:

> *"What are we to understand by this being which wills to hold itself in awe, to be at a distance from itself? Is it a question of bad faith or of another fundamental attitude? And can one live this new aspect of being? In particular will freedom by taking itself for an end escape all situation? Or will it situate itself so much the more precisely and the more individually as it projects itself further in anguish as a conditioned freedom and accepts more fully its responsibility as an existent by whom the world comes into being?"*

This is where the rubber hits the road (so to speak). Sartre could not disentangle the nature of freedom as a separate entity.

He could not explain the role of value in inciting freedom. He notes, "All these questions, which refer us to a pure and not an accessory reflection, can find their reply only on the ethical plane."[9]

Sartre concluded this piece of literature by promising to answer the previously noted questions in a future publication. He writes, "We shall devote to them a future work." As already noted, Sartre never published this work himself.

The previous understanding is the essence of the current debate over Sartre's role as a moral philosopher. Indeed, Sartre did not have the chance to publish any written work about ethics. But this argument is only accurate when considering that Sartre did not [personally] publish the materials; at least, he did not do so himself or while alive.

Sartre devoted a good portion of his time to honor his promise. He entrenched himself in long-winded writing project, which he eventually abandoned. Sartre compiled many writings about ethics.

Critics see no use for such materials. These publications are incapable of projecting Sartre into the stratosphere of a moral philosopher, they say. I reject any positions that deny Sartre a role in moral philosophy. Therefore, this book is important. It defends Jean-Paul Sartre as a moral philosopher.

The materials, which Sartre produced, commentators are positive, are incomplete. But that alone should not provide a license to critics to devalue the intellectual worth of the essays, which Sartre compiled about ethics altogether. This is the nature of the defense, which I outline in later pages.

CHAPTER 2: EXAMINING UNFAIR CRITICISMS

THE IMPORTANCE OF CRITICISMS

Most criticisms against Sartrean ethics are rash. Many of them lack a clear sense of purpose. I am not sure what commentators are after, when they refute Sartrean ethics altogether.

Everyone is entitled to his or her opinion. People may have many reasons to disagree with the gist of Sartrean ethics. I am not here to refute that reality. In the same vein, I do not offer a fanatical defense of Jean-Paul Sartre. I did not compile this book to present a blinded defense of his views about ethics. This is my way of saying that I do not rebuff dissenting opinions senselessly here.

In defending Sartrean ethics, I am not suggesting that everyone should agree with his approach to ethics in general. There are flaws in that ethics. I disagree with the way that analysts rebuke Sartre's literary imprints. Most criticisms come across (at least to me) as unwarranted. Some contentions suggest that Sartre had no idea of what he was doing.

By relying on the present discourse, one would think that Sartre fell short of proving his identity as a moral philosopher. As a result, his overall intellectual worth is questionable. His views on other issues are the center of criticisms. Critics suggest that Sartre's posthumous writings, notably the ones he compiled about ethics, are worthless. Ouch! This is harsh.

I do not see Sartre under a similar prism. I do not think his intellectual capital should be the subject of scrutiny at all. Of course, it is not clear whether this work alone would be enough to turn the debate in a different direction.

I am not a Sartrean scholar. Thus, I could not rely on this work [on its own] to defend Jean-Paul Sartre. But I must confess that I have a hard time taking criticisms against Sartrean ethics seriously. I cannot see the weight of certain arguments, which purport to refute the role, which Sartre "Supposedly," they say, played in ethics.

When critics (including, scholars, pundits, commentators, or analysts) claim that Sartrean ethics is nonexistent, I could not but wonder what is it that they meant to say. When critics claim that Sartrean ethics is incomplete, I do not see the relevance of such a view. I could not make sense of what they are trying to accomplish; at least, not in substance. Even Sartre accepted that his writings are uncompleted. This is like beating a dead horse.

Certain facets of Sartrean ethics are worthy of further analysis. I would like to discover them. But fewer investigations examined whether it was necessary for Sartre to publish a book about ethics. What I am trying to say here is that no one knows why Sartre abandoned his literary projects about ethics.

Most critics are baffled about the reason(s) Sartre failed to have a single manuscript ready for publication before his death. The literature is filled with arguments that claim to explain why Sartre failed in his promise. But these arguments exhibit speculations about the reason Sartre's literary projects are uncompleted. I am not convinced that such a scrutiny deserves a place in the debate.

Finding out the reason Sartre failed to honor his promise in ethics warrants a sensible approach. It is best to understand the man. Before exploring his views, it is important to examine the issues that affected his intellectual legacy. Critics could have focused on other elements of Sartrean ethics.

It makes sense to afford a deeper scrutiny of Sartrean ethics. It is important to examine Sartre's positions before rebuking them. But fewer publications have taken a similar approach. The consensus is that Sartrean ethics has little or no intellectual bearing. I disagree.

Many of the compilations, which criticize Sartrean ethics are one-dimensional. Facets of them are laden with bias. They are jumbled; they are filled with subjective disputations. Such editions lack a clear sense of orientation about their true purpose.

The disagreements that are levied against Sartre are uncalled for. It is difficult to take such criticisms seriously. Few analysts offer a concise rebuttal to the notion that ethics and existentialism share the same theoretical foundation. I am doubtful about criticisms.

Any argument that refutes a link between existentialism and ethics is in error. Such an approach is always in futility. That is the case, unless critics seek a destruction of Sartrean philosophy by refuting his approach to both human ontology and morality. I am perplexed of views echoed by critics who seem determined to undermine Sartre both intellectually and personally. I am concerned by positions that are too arbitrary or excessively radical. I am inclined to refute views that deny Sartre any role in moral philosophy. I am cynical of rigid positions against Sartrean ethics.

To what extent criticisms against Sartre are relevant? To what extent Sartre deserves the scrutiny that he often receives. Let us examine Sartre's true role in the ethical discipline to make sense of it all.

Chapter Notes

[1] A systematic approach means a sound process. A method or procedure designed to assess the feasibility or the viability of a task. In this instance, the task would be to develop an approach that would allow the examination of the nature or the extent of Sartrean ethics.

[2] "What Is Systematic Approach? Definition and Meaning."

[3] A system approach usually involves a process that can help gauge inconsistencies within the literature. Presently, there is no consistency in the literature. There is not a single manner to explore Sartre's moral thoughts. Examinations of that ethics are the results of speculations and inferences.

[4] Several studies about Sartre have been conducted by using methods and study designs. Such studies often take many forms. Findings often stem from many facets. Criticisms against Sartrean ethics are often the results of preconceived notions, which are often debated within the literature.

[5] Sartre, *Existentialism and Human Emotion*. David Pellauer believes that it is possible that Sartre's major work in ethics is yet to be revealed. It is not clear the extent of Sartrean ethics.

[6] Sartre, *Notebooks for an Ethics*; Detmer, "Review"; Linsenbard, *An Investigation of Jean-Paul Sartre's Posthumously Published Notebooks for an Ethics*. The Notebooks for an Ethics was originally published in 1983, posthumously.

[7] Sartre, *Being and Nothingness*, 797.

[8] Ibid.

[9] Ibid., 798.

Chapter Three

Posthumous Works

This chapter assesses the extent of Sartre's posthumous writings. They include materials published on Sartre's behalf and compilations, which have not been released to the public. The chapter examines Sartre's possible motives when he compiled these works. The chapter assesses the extent to which commentators ignore the gist of Sartrean ethics. It elaborates on how to defend Sartrean ethics. It lays out how to make the case to refute misguided criticisms against Sartre. The chapter notes that Jean-Paul Sartre could be considered a pseudo-moral philosopher.

CHAPTER

3

Assessing Sartre's True Intent

Most observers do not understand the reason many of Sartre's literary contributions, notably the ones that he produced about ethics, are unfinished or fragmented. This confusion is interesting. There is no doubt that these works are uncompleted. This fact, at least, universally speaking, is undisputable.

There is no need to continue debating this argument. There is no need to debate the intellectual relevance of Sartre's posthumous writings. To reiterate, Sartre admitted that his ideas were underdeveloped. He recognized that facets of these materials are obscure. Any dispute about the fragmentary nature of these

Chapter 3: Examining Sartre's True Intent

editions is unnecessary. This fact should be considered a minor detail. Else, it should be considered a non-issue. But this is not what is plain to see in the current literary discourse about Sartrean ethics.

As established in the last two chapters, Sartre did not publish his works about ethics. It is also a known fact that Sartre did not complete most of his projects about the subject. As we will illustrate further in the manuscript, Sartre said so himself. Then, what is the point of the debate? I am lost.

Moreover, it is not a secret that the materials, which Sartre purportedly produced about ethics were released [on his behalf] postmortem. Also, they were released in their original format, which Sartre himself insisted to happen in a similar fashion before his passing. Then again, what is the reason for the back and forth in the literature about those works?

As is usual, critics have rarely ignored the opportunity to appeal to the reality [so mentioned above] to undermine Sartre's publications in ethics. But this minor detail [I would say] seems to provide enough motivation to critics to admonish Sartre personally. But do they have an ulterior motive? That, I am not sure.

Most critical publications against Sartrean ethics always mention that Sartre's literary projects are fragmented. It is as if Sartre were everything but a real philosopher. This is simply because he fell short of completing his works about ethics. This is laughable.

In addition, critics often point out that Sartre did not publish his own works. Apparently, not publishing one's works is a *no-no* in contemporary literature. This is as if to imply that whatever is out there, whether it is attached to Sartre's name, is inauthentic. Critics use this peculiarity as a testament of Sartre's intellectual failing in the ethical domain. This is absurd.

In effect, Sartre died without returning to his abandoned projects. There is no need to explicate what led him to abandon them in the first place. I do not know the « *raison d'être* » for his decision. No one knows why that is. I could not explain what situation or events, which prevented Sartre from completing his writings.

It is worthy of note that, even though Sartre discarded many of his compilations about human morality, he did not abandon his interests in ethics. Every reality suggests that Sartre was aware of the possibility that parts [or the whole] of his collected works, significantly the materials that he produced about ethics, might be unfinished on his death. He also knew that they might be published as is.

Arlette Elkaïm-Sartre Clarifies

Sartre was not concerned with the way commentators might react to his essays. He was satisfied with the possibility that those materials might be published postmortem. Sartre was glad of that prospect; he expected such a possibility.

Elkaïm-Sartre, notes that Sartre expected his philosophical materials, notably the ones he produced about ethics, would be published after his death.[1] Sartre was looking forward to having his writings released to the public, however fragmented they might be. Sartre explained his views about the future of his uncompleted materials. In the Situation X (1975), Sartre writes:

« *Ils représenteront ce que, à un moment donné, j'ai voulu faire et que j'ai renoncé à terminer, et c'est définitif. Tandis que, tant que je suis vivant…, il reste une possibilité que je les reprenne ou que je dise en quelques mots ce que je voulais en faire. Publiés après ma mort, ces textes restent inachevés, tels qu'ils sont, obscurs, puisque j'y formule*

Chapter 3: Examining Sartre's True Intent

des idées qui ne sont pas toutes développées. Ce sera au lecteur d'interpréter où elles auraient pu me mener ».

Translation:

"These materials will represent, at the right time, what I wanted to do and decided to abandon definitively. So long as I am alive…, there is always the possibility that I might reconsider completing them and say in a few words what I sought to carry out in them. But if they were to be published after my death, these texts should remain as is, uncompleted, and obscure, mainly because most of the ideas I developed in them are not developed. It will be left to the reader to decipher where those ideas would have taken me."

(J.-P. Sartre, *Situations X*, 1975, as noted in « *Cahiers pour une morale* » page 7).

Sartre recognizes that his unfinished materials were obscure. But he did not suggest that they were inconsequential as an intellectual device to decipher his ethics; he did not hint that they were incomprehensible. Suggesting otherwise is misguided. Sartre did not insinuate that his works lacked a theoretical scheme. Sartre seemed confident that the reader would be able to decipher what he sought to carry out in them.

Sartre did not envisage that his literary accomplishments would be set aside because of their incompleteness. The concession that Sartre failed to complete most of his texts about ethics does not nullify such works. This fact should not provide a license to commentators to minimize the intellectual worth of these publications.

The previous quote could be interpreted to mean that Sartre had a clear trajectory in mind when he decided to abandon his project about ethics. Despite everything that critics said, Sartre had been working on his views about ethics long before developing his theory about existentialism. Still, the questions remain the same.

Why did Sartre abandon his ideas about ethics? Why did Sartre concentrate most of his time exploring human ontology? Subsequent chapters provide insightful explanations about that.

I do not delve in depth in the reason Sartre, they say, chose to work on phenomenological ontology rather than continuing to expand on his moral thoughts. But one could speculate about the potential motives, which might have led Sartre to this decision. In following portions of the manuscript, I explore these questions with more interest.

It is necessary to provide seminal answers about the extent to which Jean-Paul Sartre deserves credit for his posthumous releases. Even though most of Sartre's manuscripts are unfinished, he earned his recognition as a contributor in this literary discipline. Criticisms, I argue here, appear guided by mistaken assumptions about the man, his moral views, and his philosophy.

Making the previous claim is not a desperate attempt to provide a needless defense for Sartre or for his ethics. It is not a ploy to satisfy my hubris. It is not embroidery of my analytical prowess.

This book is not designed to brag about my capacity to analyze dense concepts. It is not intended to come across as excessively confident about the effects that such a work might have in the present discourse or in the literature about Sartrean ethics. But it is worth noting that the tide is against Sartre.

Somebody ought to defend Jean-Paul Sartre. This great philosopher deserves better than the treatments that he is currently receiving from literary critics from all over the world. Sartre is pummeled; he is admonished; he is derided; he is vilified from all possible angles. That is simply not right.

Criticisms about Sartrean ethics are unremitting and vicious. They are without reprieve. Sartre, one could say, gained more relevance in the literature through criticisms, as opposed to the

Chapter 3: Examining Sartre's True Intent

valor of his collected works or his contributions to human literature. The present work is intended to incite a positive change in this regard.

Outlining My Goals

Ethics is not an easy subject to decipher. Ethical issues are not always malleable. The term ethics underlies a broad concept. But this work does not assess this concept in depth.

Examining Sartre's thoughts about ethics could be cumbersome. Even though Sartrean philosophy is hugely popular, the same could not be said about his views concerning his approach to ethics. From here, this task is proportionally challenging.

In most literary circles, the types of materials Jean-Paul Sartre consistently produced are considered high-end intellectual products. As a skillful writer and a prominent thinker, Sartre is well read. Ronald Aronson and Adrian van den Hoven note, "Sartre's work and ideas are very much with us today."[2]

Sartrean thoughts in a wide range of topics are still relevant in modern literature. Yet, the nature of Sartrean philosophy, let alone his moral views, is not well understood.[3] Why that is the case?

Critics have rejected the idea that Sartrean philosophy could be considered urbane. The consensus is similar when it comes to his approach to ethics. The common view is that both published and unpublished texts about moral philosophy do not justify Sartre the status of a prominent contributor in this discipline.

For others, the Sartrean impetus in ethics has little or no intellectual bearing. Such compilations, analysts echoed, have little or no literary worth. I reject arguments that rely on such a view.

I would admit that Sartre's ideas about ethics are not always consistent. Indeed, his posthumous manuscripts also appear fragmented. But while observers are inclined to regard these editions as lacking in centrality, I see them as points of reference. They could allow us to appreciate the nature of Sartre's intellectual identity in moral philosophy.

I do not subscribe to viewpoints, which assume that Sartre's writings lack an ethical ingredient. I do not support arguments that reject Sartre's publications without a thorough scrutiny of their contents. I do not share disputes that reject Sartre's role in ethics simply because his contributions in moral philosophy, they say, are incomplete or disjointed. I do not share positions that seem slanted against Sartre. There is a need to refute popular claims about Sartrean philosophy. They are, in my view, too biased, which makes them shamelessly misguided.

Refuting the Arguments

No question about it; Sartre was not successful in laying out his moral beliefs. He could not carry his views in a coherent format. The question is whether this is reason enough to rebuke Sartrean ethics altogether. I would say no.

Except of Sartre's notebooks, there exist little or no other published versions about his assessment of certain ethical issues. Few inquiries have examined the weight of the Sartrean approach to ethics. Little publications have examined Sartre's moral thoughts from a neutral perspective.

Views are mitigated. Inquirers approach the issues with preconceived notions. Critics examine the nature of Sartrean ethics deductively. They often overlook certain phases of that ethics. Perhaps they rely so much on false assumptions about that ethics.

CHAPTER 3: EXAMINING SARTRE'S TRUE INTENT

The views they often echo about Sartre reflect their own bias toward the man. Their positions often grow out of rigid notions about Sartre. The common deduction from their approach is that Sartre's publications have no intellectual substance.

Critics echoed that Sartrean ethics is lacking any theoretical foundation. Sartre has no intellectual relevance in moral philosophy, they say. But this is hardly the case. There is more to the Sartrean model to ethics than most would admit.

Most observers have not taken the time to appreciate Sartre's contribution. Whether this is because Sartre is a controversial figure is not clear. It is irrefutable that a side of Sartrean ethics has not been cultivated by most inquirers. Few people have a clear sense of Sartrean ethics.

Even though I might be unable to change the present debate, the mere effort to propose a balanced viewpoint is a step in the right direction. The Sartrean approach to ethics is often rebuked without mercy. Sartre is seldom treated [justly] in the literature.

Critics are likely to rebuff Sartrean ethics. They often do so by evoking several reasons, many of which are one-sided. Most inquiries about Sartre are laden with unnecessary conclusions. There is a need to draw a line in the debate. There is a need to take a stand in Sartre's defense no matter how superfluous they might seem to some observers or no matter how inconsequential such a defense might sound to those who consider themselves intellectually worthier than Jean-Paul Sartre.

INCONSISTENT CRITICISMS

When commentators say that Sartre did not produce any large body of works about ethics, while recognizing that he produced several other publications in the field, this is a flagrant attack against the man. Such attacks are always subjective. They do not help the present conversation. I would say that the term *substantial* has no merit. It delineates personal interpretations about a subject or a person. The same is true when we are talking about the works, which Sartre produced about ethics. Stating that such works are not *substantial* has no real meaning. Making such a claim does not change the nature of the works, which clearly delineate Sartrean ethics.

The term *substantial* does not provide any information about the extent of Sartre's contribution in ethics. It is no more than an arbitrary way of cataloging Sartre's literary valor. This term is evoked to lessen Sartre's literary contributions in the field. It is perhaps a way to devalue Sartre himself.

How many books philosophers like Plato, Aristotle, John Locke, and Jeremy Bentham, just to name a few, produced or published, which had been unambiguously tailored for ethics? You might be surprised to find out that, by comparison, Sartre produced more materials about ethics than these philosophers did. Yet, many of these thinkers are famous for their ideas about ethics. But Sartre's legitimacy in the field is often the subject of intense scrutiny.

Few analysts would voice support for Sartre in the ethical domain. Why there is a double standard? I am not sure how to answer. Nonetheless, there is a need for a different perspective in the debate about the role Jean-Paul Sartre played in ethics.

Here, I propose an inductive approach.[4] Instead of exploring Sartre's writings from one standpoint (deductively), it might be necessary to examine those thoughts inductively. That way, it would be easier to cater a better understanding from them.[5] Such an approach, I am certain, would prevent unnecessary bias from the analysis. It would allow an evaluation of Sartre's take on ethics by exploring his major editions in the field.

Chapter 3: Examining Sartre's True Intent

Examining a philosophical issue is not the same as exploring a social event. Of course, I am not suggesting that we should treat Sartrean philosophy as a social event. But it is worthy of note that the Sartrean approach to human morality has an undeniable social component. The moral agent (the being) is unmistakable in the views, which Sartre expressed in many of his publications. It is necessary to evaluate Sartrean ethics out of a scrutiny of the content of his works.

There is a need to avoid examining Sartre's publications expediently. There is a need to focus on the quality of such materials and not necessarily on their quantity. We should not ignore the marrow of the contentions against these collections, for they reflect impulsive, if not, irrational viewpoints.

Is it necessary to approach a philosophical topic inductively?[6] The answer is yes. When it comes to Sartre, there is always a reason to examine his manuscripts about ethics inductively. However, since claims are often slanted against him, it might be difficult, if not impossible, to have a good grasp of his approach without weeding out destructive criticisms.

An inductive approach is the best way to assess the extent of Sartrean ethics. The information that we examine must come from an inductive process. An inductive approach would yield productive criticisms. There is a need to approach Sartrean ethics holistically. Investigations must be construed inductively.

Yes, Sartre was a contentious thinker. But much of the controversies about his theses, outstandingly the oppositions about his moral thoughts, are unfounded. We must examine Sartrean ethics differently from the way inquirers have approached these issues in the past. Instead of confirming preconceived notions about Sartre and his literary achievements, it might be more productive to let these materials speak for themselves. This approach might allow a thorough scrutiny of Sartre's intellectual valor in ethics.

I have adopted a similar stance in this text. I am convinced this is the best way to provoke a real debate about Sartrean ethics. This approach is the only way to balance out inconsistencies in the literature. It is a way to set aside criticisms, which are trivial.

Denying Sartrean Ethics

It is worthy of note that it is not a secret that many commentators do not like Sartre's approach to moral philosophy. They are so caught up in their contempt for the man on a personal level that they effortlessly overlook the value of his intellectual legacy. For these critics, there is always a need to refute Sartrean ethics.

Aronson and Hoven note that "Scoring points against a man who exposed most of his life to the public gaze is not difficult."[7] There is a line between refuting the writer himself and refuting his ideas. With Jean-Paul Sartre, his avid critics refute both. I do not understand why.

I do not agree with the gist of existentialism. But I would not refute Sartre's intellectual relevance in phenomenology. Suppose that Sartre had concretized his project for an ethics and had he defended his stance against criticisms, commentators would still find a way to reject his position. This is my understanding of the current debate.

As you navigate this book, two important questions are worth considering. What led Sartre to abandon his texts about ethics? Is it possible that Sartre was wary of criticisms when he decided to parse his ideas about ethics? I am not sure what his motivations were.

Chapter 3: Examining Sartre's True Intent

Nobody knows why Sartre took another direction in his original goal to decipher the moral agent to build individual values. It is not clear why Sartre abandoned his pursuit to disentangle human freedom with morality. Why did he make that choice, even though he promised his readers to dedicate a future work to ethics? We could speculate about potential reasons.

Sartre did not have to echo his moral concerns independently from phenomenological ontology. Yet, he chose to do just that. Why he made that choice in that specific juncture of his career. Again, answers are not clear.

There was no point in debating ethics separately from existentialism. Sartre did not have to expand the ideas he advanced about human ontology on the ethical plane. Such ideas were already plain in the arguments he echoed about freedom.

There is a need to focus on the views that Sartre echoed in the book titled *Being and Nothingness* to make the case for Sartrean ethics. This text examines that ethics from the lens of existentialism.

In the book « *Cahiers pour une morale,* » for instance, Sartre argued that ethics was intrinsic within phenomenological ontology. In the aforementioned publication, he writes:

> « La moralité devient un certain mode d'être ontologique et même métaphysique auquel il nous faut atteindre ».[8]

Translation:

> "Ethics becomes an ontological modality and even metaphysical, which we must achieve."

In the above quote, Sartre shows that morality and human ontology are distinct ideas. One could also make the case that similar viewpoints would be apparent if examined from the same perspective. They could be approached from an individual prism.

Ethics is an individual goal, which is closely intertwined with human ontology. Every being must concretize an ethics. This becomes an ontological priority or even a supernatural need.

Sartrean ethics is known as *"Existentialist Ethics."* It seems as though Sartre detached freedom from ethics only for analytical purposes. These two concepts go hand in hand. From now on, ethics and ontology could be examined in tandem. I adopt a similar scheme from beginning to end.

Critics do not see a relationship between ontology and morality. Richard Bernstein, for instance, notes that in *"l'Existentialisme est un humanisme,"* freedom is without question a moral concept—but the chasm between the ontology and moral is an unbridgeable one.[10] Other observers point out the presence of ambiguities in the types of examination to ethics Sartre proposed.

Most observers tie Sartre's commonly admitted meager contribution to ethics as a testament of his limited intellectual merit in the field or the lack of that. I dispute that viewpoint. Ethical notions, I argue, are entrenched in Sartrean philosophy. There could not be one (ethics) without the other (human ontology). We could not examine Sartrean ethics in a vacuum.

Pseudo-Moral Philosopher

Sartre is a moral philosopher. As a comfort, however, he could be considered a *Pseudo-Moral-Philosopher*. So long as his ethical views are intertwined with phenomenological ontology. Sartre's approach to morality needs not be distinctly described from human ontology to settle its significance. Trying to demarcate the two concepts as separate entities is the wrong way to understand their essence.

I cannot defend Sartre by any stretch of the imagination. I lack the intellectual background to respond efficaciously to the points of disagreements, which are often advanced [callously, I might add] in the literature. But via this publication, I hope to encourage a better examination of Sartre's overall inputs in ethics.

Despite the noted limits, my approach might help the reader make sense of the growing debate. This work could be helpful to the literature. All the same, it might help widen the scope of the conversation about Sartre. It might help explain the reach of Sartrean ethics. I might interject a novel point of departure in the current discourse.

This work includes several unpublished works, which had been released by Arlette Elkaïm-Sartre and properly credited to Jean-Paul Sartre. It examines the views voiced by several scholars, many of whom have intimated themselves with Sartre's publications over the years. Before we continue in examining the gist of the debate, let us explore the intricacies of the issues that pervade the literature. Let us explore the extent of Sartrean ethics. Let us assess the nature of the debate. Let us evaluate the extent to which analysts have a genuine reason to refute Sartrean ethics.

The next few chapters evaluate the extent of Sartrean ethics. But the analysis echoed in them is broad. These chapters explore the issues from various angles. They summarize the arguments that are regularly repeated in the literature.

Chapter Notes

[1] Sartre, *Cahiers pour une morale*.

[2] Aronson and Hoven, *Sartre Alive*, 11.

[3] Detmer, *Freedom as a Value*.

[4] Is there a clear distinction between inductive and deductive reasoning? The answer is yes.

[5] "Deduction & Induction."

⁶ Deductive reasoning usually begins with a theory or set of theories, which via a hypothesis aid observation, the researcher is seeking to confirm. Inductive reasoning, on the other hand, is the mirror approach. In this instance, the researcher sees and look for patterns to establish a hypothesis and ultimately develop a theory.

In the case of Sartrean ethics, inquirers usually approach the topic with a particular theory in mind. They are only seeking to confirm that theory. Most of the time, their theory comes from erroneous assumptions about Sartre and his approach to the subject.

I propose a different approach. Instead of looking at Sartrean ethics from a particular prism, it might be best to examine the compilations, which Sartre produced holistically. That way, it might be possible to afford them the fairest possible scrutiny. I am convinced that such an approach would reveal that Sartrean ethics is not that elusive, as critics have echoed in the literature.

⁷ Aronson and Hoven, *Sartre Alive*, 25.

⁸ Sartre, *Cahiers pour une morale*, 11.

⁹ Anderson, "Beyond Sartre's Ethics of Authenticity."

¹⁰ Bernstein, *Praxis and Action*, 154.

Chapter 3: Examining Sartre's True Intent

CHAPTER FOUR

Developing a Technique

This chapter elaborates on the scheme I used to review the available materials. It relates popular suppositions about the term ethics. It examines the reason it is necessary to assess the Sartrean approach to moral philosophy from a different angle. This chapter explains the limits of the arguments shown in the text. It focuses on disparaging approaches, which permeate the current debate. The chapter lays out the preferred approach to defend Sartrean ethics. It sums up the chosen theoretical scheme.

CHAPTER

4

EXAMINING SARTREAN ETHICS

What would be the best way to examine Sartrean ethics? Finding a succinct answer might be hard. At first, I wanted to consider several approaches. I wanted to devise a new way to compare Jean-Paul Sartre's writings with the publications produced by other, perhaps more prominent, philosophers. This approach proved complicated.

Examining the issues from this lens presumed that ethics could be understood from a universal lens. But this is not the case. Let us explore the term ethics further.

Chapter 4: Examining Sartrean Ethics

The term ethics is a blanket terminology; it usually notes virtue. There exists fewer or no approach, which could explain this concept differently. Various schools of thought claim to explicate how human ontology works. Observers claim to sketch the term, principally when it comes to notions of *deontology* and *morality*. Nonetheless, philosophers rarely take similar approaches when they examine complex ethical issues.

No doubt, ethical principles exist in Sartrean philosophy. For instance, in the publication titled *"Notebooks for an Ethics,"* Sartre proved beyond any doubt that he was a thinker worthy of an ethical recognition. This is true at least within the context of the French tradition of the expression known as « *Le Moraliste* » or *"The Moralist."*[1] Despite views to the contrary, Sartre proved his moral concerns within the context of French literary traditions.

The deduction in most literary circles is that there is a universality in the way ethical issues could be assessed. Nevertheless, I do not dispute the uniformity argument. Scholars often evoked universal principles when they examine ethical issues.

A universal approach to ethics is useful when examining abstract principles. For example, when scholars discuss ethical concerns or when they evaluate issues that have ethical tentacles, it is not always obvious whether their scrutiny comes from abstract perceptions or concrete understandings. Even so, there is a need for a different approach when examining the extent of Sartrean ethics.

When it comes to Sartrean ethics, an irrefutable crack exists between abstract and concrete rules. The way Sartre approaches ethical issues is geared more toward the latter rather than the former. Sartrean ethics is more realistic; it is grounded in human reality.

I agree, at least to some extent, that ethics could be examined differently. But such rules could be studied from a specific angle as well. Ethics could be understood as a trade (profession); it could emerge from a social condition or a social injustice (justice). It could come forth a caring attitude (care). It could also evolve out of an evaluation of a particular social reality (critique). See the publication titled *Jean-Paul Sartre: A Legacy Under Attack* to learn more about these concepts.

The term ethics is a subjective concept. Ethical issues concern one individual. One person could not be held responsible, morally, or perhaps legally as well, for the actions, which are posed by another person. For instance, I may not be responsible for actions posed by people who are not directly under my *govern* or control.

Morality is the affair of the individual, even if morally inspired behaviors are governed by society or even though such comportments might be influenced by community settings. That is why examining ethical issues often entail descriptors, such as *Morality*. Such a descriptor entails notions, such as the following: *Values, Norms,* and *Traditions*. Other rules, mostly notions about *Reason*, might be included. Such descriptors could be understood universally.

The principles referenced earlier encompass inferences about the term virtue (*right* and *wrong*). The individual may choose to engage in conducts that might be considered right or wrong by society. From a Sartrean lens, freedom allows the being the capacity to decide which course of action is correct in a particular circumstance.

One could not speak of human ontology without referencing human ethics. Sartre seldom reflected on notions of virtue in his lines. He does not mention the term morality specifically when he examines the being via phenomenological ontology. However, examining Sartrean ethics in this manner proved exceedingly difficult.

CHAPTER 4: EXAMINING SARTREAN ETHICS

How could I be certain that ethical notions play a crucial role in Sartrean philosophy? While I do not have a clear answer, I could evoke the last paragraphs in *Being and Nothingness* to point out that Sartre clearly proposed such a link in his works. Perhaps this is the reason that led him to promise to dedicate a future project to ethics.

My grasp of the issues will become obvious as I decipher Sartre and his views about ethics. My position will make more sense when I develop my understanding of Sartrean philosophy. This book will make sense when I examine criticisms against the Sartrean approach to morality.

My defense of Sartrean ethics will make sense as I assess Sartre's conceivable purposes, especially when he expressed his concerns about ethics in the posthumously released items. There is a need to explore Sartre's possible intents in compiling these works. But I do so mainly by examining his contributions to moral philosophy.

Before we delve in the gist of the issues, let me elaborate on the means I used as a theoretical scheme. Let me explain the technique I used to examine Sartre's true impact on ethics. Let me clarify the crux of Sartrean ethics.

SEARCHING FOR A METHOD

Completing this project was daunting. I could not come up with the right technique to study the topic. I wanted to review as many contentions about Sartrean philosophy as possible. But I found it almost impossible to locate viewpoints that echoed a balanced approach.

I was interested in materials, which Sartre produced himself or materials Sartre is credited to have produced about ethics. Doing so was incredibly challenging. I could not locate such materials.

Two reasons are worth pointing out. First, locating relevant texts about Sartre was nearly impossible. As I delved in the investigation, it became clear that known publications might not provide enough information to conduct a methodical assessment of Sartrean ethics.

The second reason, which posed a challenge to conducting the proper investigation about Sartrean ethics, is related to having access to the known materials. Understandings about Sartrean ethics are the results of a few mentions here and there in the literature. Most of the materials (released postmortem), which Sartre is credited to have *produced* are not readily accessible for public scrutiny. Thus, most of Sartre's unpublished materials about ethics were not available to conduct a primary analysis of those documents.

While it was impossible to examine Sartre's recently released publications firsthand, that did not mean that the materials were off limits. That did not mean that such works were inconsequential for completing my investigation. I realized that I had to be creative in my investigative techniques.

I knew that Sartre had *produced* several materials about ethics.[2] I knew that some people had access to them. Of course, these materials do not offer enough evidence to support the notion that Sartre is a great writer in ethics. But they peeked my interests. I wanted to have, at least, a brief look of these items.

In the beginning, I was animated with the need to assess these works myself. I was eager to review excerpts from them. I wanted to have access to these works even if I might have to do so incrementally. But I had to accept my logistical limits.

Limits

Although Sartre produced several compilations about his ethics, most of these items is unknown. They are not available to the public. Elkaïm-Sartre has propriety over those materials. She decides when [or how] they can be accessed. Since most of the materials Sartre produced had not been published or released to literary groups or to other settings (such as a library or a museum), it was fitting to rely on the views voiced by those who had examined them.

I wanted to locate as many of Sartre's publications as possible. I wanted to review them. That was the best way, I thought, I could evaluate their content. But this goal was frustrated for the same reasons mentioned earlier. It was impossible to access the posthumously released materials.

Despite the noted limits, I found an expedient way to examine the epitome of Sartrean ethics. I realized that there is a link between ethics and phenomenology. I wanted to explore that relationship further.

Since most of the ideas that Sartre echoed in his works about existentialism are sketched in his [already] published and [widely available] materials, it was obvious that locating them would not pose a serious challenge. I wanted to gain valuable insights from these publications. They became the basis of my analysis here.

It could be difficult to detach ethical notions from Sartrean philosophy. It could be impossible to remove ethics from existentialism. As I reviewed the other works, which Sartre produced about human ontology, I realized that describing the essence of Sartrean ethics was not that difficult after all.

A few limits are still worthy of mention here. For instance, I could not encapsulate the extent of Sartre's publications in the ethical domain. Nonetheless, I knew that Sartre had an uncanny need to unravel the individual (or the being) as a separate entity in the world. I concluded that a Sartrean approach to morality could be understood as an unrestricted need to evaluate the man in his most intimate state.

In the existentialist model, the being is the centerpiece of scrutiny. He is constantly the object of intense introspection. I expected a similar approach in Sartre's exploration of ethical issues.

I wanted to examine the role of ontology in Sartrean ethics. I wanted to evaluate the intellectual foundation of phenomenology. But I had to center my analysis on the ideas, which Sartre proposed in his most famous texts about existentialism. Therefore, I focused on the ideas that Sartre echoed in *Being and Nothingness*.

Many scholars examined outstanding qualities of Sartre's published works—perhaps his unpublished materials as well—haphazardly. Critics focused only on the ethical portions of his essays, while others sought to capture a broader scope of his views. Few scholars conducted a rigorous assessment of Sartre's role in ethics. Most analysts approached the Sartrean contribution to ethics superficially.

Most arguments debating Sartre's role in the ethical domain are one-sided. But other examinations, although a handful, are neutral. Some offer mixed criticisms of Sartrean ethics. I decided to conduct a secondary analysis of existing data about Sartrean ethics.

I located the publications of three scholars who are familiar with Sartrean ethics. They have a similarity in the way that they approach Sartre's ideas about the subject. These editions served as a point of reference for the views I echo from this point forward.

My early analysis relates the viewpoints featured in two major texts. They include *Sartre Alive* (1991) and *Sartre's Two Ethics: From Authenticity to Integral Humanity* (1993). Keep in mind that my views come from the hope that I could help settle points of strife in the literature about Sartrean ethics. I wanted to bridge the gap between

Chapter 4: Examining Sartrean Ethics

those who are convinced that Sartre played no role in moral philosophy and those who believe that a Sartrean ethics exist, though in its early stage, fragmented, or uncompleted. I prone a simplistic approach to understand the extent of that ethics.

A Simplistic Approach

The best way to examine criticisms against Sartrean ethics is through the lens of existing literature. There is not a scarcity of discussions about the nature of that ethics. Surely, the literature is not settled about Sartre's take on ethical issues. Since several scholars have written extensively about Sartrean ethics, my goal was to locate such edition. I wanted to explore these arguments in depth.

Apart from a tight circle of commentators, there is not a common understanding about the gist of Sartrean ethics. Even within that circle of analysts, views often diverge, chiefly when it comes to the impact Sartre might have had in the field. Positions are scattered on this issue.

Those who oppose the idea that Sartre had any relevance in ethical writings could be hard to convince otherwise. Of course, other commentators, though relatively in small numbers, might be opened to embrace a different approach. It would not be far-fetched to try to convert a few skeptics.

A few observers, Sartrean scholars, do not make it clear whether they might support the notion that Sartre should be considered a moral philosopher. Few people support the notion that Sartre's essays have literary value in ethics. But the writings presented here are not dedicated to changing that reality. There is little expectation that such a work would make a huge difference in the debate.

Most critics nourish preconceived notions about Sartre. Others are blatantly biased when examining the Sartrean approach to morality. It might be difficult, if not impossible, to change opinions about the man, let alone his paperbacks. The goal of this volume is to offer a different approach to the issues.

There is a need to settle the fissure, which plagues the debate. Whether this is feasible remains to be seen. I suppose it is worthy of a trial.

I hope to echo the views espoused by those who support the possibility that a Sartrean ethics exists and those who reject that prospect. Sartre deserves credits for creating or for trying to create—depending on which side of the debate one stands—a great ethical foundation in his works. The challenge is to provide evidence to support that claim as convincingly as possible.

Examining Posthumous Works

During his literary career, Sartre produced several materials, which relayed his views about human ontology. Until the early 1980s and even during the mid-1990s, it was commonly understood that Jean-Paul Sartre was not a writer in ethics. It was widely accepted that Sartre had produced fewer titles, which sketched his ethical views.

Nowadays, it is accepted, although reluctantly, that Sartre was continually active in ethics. Obviously, there are skeptics. Critics are convinced that Sartre was not active in ethics to the point where he could be considered an authority in this discipline.

Even though many observers have questioned Sartre's literary relevance in the domain, few could deny that he produced several relevant materials in the discipline. Depriving Sartre of his rightful place as a relevant voice in ethics seems unjust. Such a deprivation could amount to an intellectual dispossession.

I will continue to echo that the foundation of Sartrean philosophy intertwines with various ethical concepts. Grasping the extent of Sartre's role in the ethical sphere is important. Nonetheless, this could only be carried out by examining the extent to which he explained his views about being in the world (human ontology). A thorough examination of existentialism, in tandem with the Sartrean approach to ethics, would be a good place to start.

I examine several facets of the issues evoked in the literature. I examine the Sartrean approach from a phenomenological lens. I explore the theoretical underpinnings of the Sartrean modes of examining ethics.

A Sartrean view about human morality could not be understood as a stand-alone project. The Sartrean slant about ethics is a part of the existentialist model. One perspective needs to be examined with others. This is the case in the most ontological sense.

Sartre developed a strong basis for his ethics. Ethical concerns make up an integral phase of the human ontological project. Sartre's publications in the ethical domain needed not be tailored as a separate field of study.

Critics do not always see a link between the two philosophical models. Critics are convinced that Sartrean philosophy and Sartrean ethics are two distinct projects. They agree that Sartre succeeded in setting up an intellectual niche via phenomenology. But when it comes to ethics, views are mitigated.

Few observers would refute that Jean-Paul Sartre could be considered the father of the existentialist model, principally when it comes to the modern slant of the existentialist paradigm. The debate is brewing about the nature of Sartrean ethics. The argument echoed by most commentators is that there is no correspondence between existentialism and ethics. I disagree with that viewpoint.

Sartrean ethics is as relevant as Sartrean philosophy. There could not be one without the other. This is the reason I offer a different perspective in the debate.

I do not share viewpoints, which insinuate, whether directly or by implication, that human ontology and morality come from a dissimilar intellectual angle. There are ample reasons to disagree with the previous understanding. In short, I refute [vehemently here] the presumption that these approaches are contradictory. The people who approach Sartrean ethics that way could be in error.

Denying a link between ontology and ethics is not a good way to explore the issues. The Sartrean ethical model could be examined from a different angle. I propose such an angle here.

Lack of Theoretical Scheme

The argument often echoed to support the notion that Sartrean has no relevance in ethical writings is that his approach is vague. Sartrean ethics, they say, does not carry any intellectual weight. Sartre's writings lack any theoretical scheme, critics often echo. How is this possible, I often wonder? The evidence points to the contrary.

I discuss the theoretical argument in greater length in the next chapter. It is worth noting that commentators often note that Sartre failed to outline the theoretical underpinnings of his approach. Let us explore the weight of this claim.

The popular viewpoint is that Sartre did not have an ethical roadmap. It is often echoed that Sartre barely made the case for his

Chapter 4: Examining Sartrean Ethics

ethical concerns in both published and unpublished materials. Critics said that Sartre came up empty in his push to develop the foundation of his moral thoughts. Another pervading viewpoint is that Sartre failed to explain a convincing argument about his potentials as a moral philosopher. I disagree with that understanding.

Critics argue that Sartre did not outline the outcomes of his approach. Sartre only developed disjointed concepts, which serve as a scheme for his ethics. Relying on that view, commentators contend that appealing to the uncompleted materials to claim that a Sartrean ethics exists is shortsighted and irresponsible. But let me offer a different side of that ethics.

It is necessary to elaborate on specific points, which symbolize Sartre's intellectual worth in the ethical domain. For example, Sartre compiled enough materials to make him a successful moral philosopher. Although I do not delve into the *nitty-gritty* of Sartre's literary works in the ethical domain, it is worth outlining the founding principles of the Sartrean postulation to moral philosophy.

The next chapters highlight striking views, which are often raised at *viva voce* against Sartrean ethics. I try to refute as many of such views as possible. I show their flaws by pointing the reason there is a need to examine the items, which Sartre produced, from a different lens.

I would admit that there is not a clear strategy to examine the extent of Sartrean ethics. But my approach consists of reviewing existing items (the literature) about Jean-Paul Sartre. I examine compilations, which refute the Sartrean ethical side. But my approach here is limited. I could not access the most prominent publications, which Sartre produced about ethics.

My thesis reflects the views expressed by several individuals, many of whom are convinced that Sartre played a role in ethics. In the same vein, my positions are limited to the views expressed by these scholars. Sadly, there are not many of them. Thus, my arguments are limited in scope. Nonetheless, that does not minimize the intellectual worth of the present volume.

Refuting Sartrean Ethics

The literature is filled with writings, which refute the scope of Sartrean ethics. Before I transition from outlining the gist of the text into examining the extent of criticisms against Sartre, let me take the time to explore, though briefly, the etymon of the term Sartrean ethics. Let me assess, although modestly here, the cogency of the concept known as Sartrean ethics. Let me examine the points of disputes that are echoed against that ethics.

The issue that observers often note is the understanding that Sartre fell short of making a compelling case for his ethics. Even in his posthumous tomes, they say, Sartre did not lay out the essence of his arguments. Critics evoke several points of contention to refute Sartrean ethics. They are as follows: the publication argument, the substance argument, and the theoretical argument.

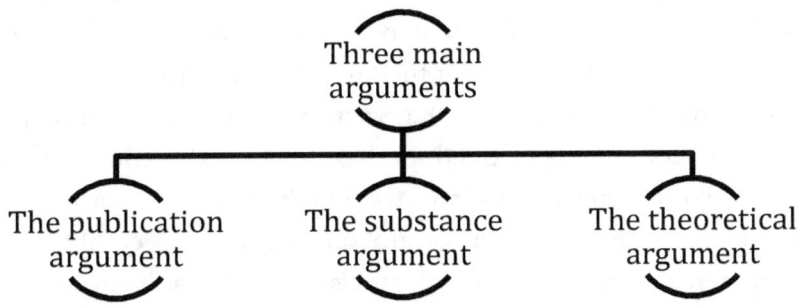

Chapter 4: Examining Sartrean Ethics

Evidently, I reject the previous contentions. They are confused, to say the least. They do not consider other interpretations about the works, which Sartre produced to reveal his approach to ethics. These arguments seldom consider that the Sartrean model to human ontology intertwines with ethics. Put differently, Sartre had a clear foundation for his ethics. That foundation could be understood as Sartre's distinct wish to understand the being in the world from an ethical lens. Sartre echoed that foundation loud and clear in his written works.

The individual (the being) construes his ethical conducts as he pleases. Members of society, in turn, reinforce such conducts. We could not speak of human ontology without meddling in human ethics, vice versa.

Sartre could be classified as both a moral philosopher and an existentialist. But commentators would probably refute that understanding. As a compromise, I would propose here, we could afford Sartre the title of a *pseudo moral thinker*. Perhaps Sartre himself would not object to that status, considering that he admitted that his collected materials on the subject are obscure and not fully developed.

Despite the previous concession, I oppose the idea that Sartre was not a moral philosopher. I reject the notion that Sartre did not compile works, which place him on the crest of moral philosophy. I would contend that the extent of Sartrean ethics is evident in every facet of his writings about the human experience.

If we were to accept that the Sartrean approach to ontology, notably his notions about freedom, has intellectual merit, then we should feel the same about his views on ethics. To me, perhaps to Sartre as well, there is little or no difference between the two approaches. I would go as far as to claim that these conceptions are interlaced. The views that Sartre echoed about freedom parallel his approach to morality. Now, how is that possible, you might be asking?

My answer is that in the Sartrean world, there is a synergetic relationship between morality and ontology. These concepts interweave in the most fundamental sense. The way the individual would go about building values, which would indisputably affect his understanding of the community where he evolves, has ethical ramifications. That reality would have undeniable ethical implications.

Chapter Notes

[1] Julian Bourg, From Revolution to Ethics: May 1968 and Contemporary French Thought (McGill-Queen's Press - MQUP, 2007).

[2] Sartre produced many materials on ethics. The materials, which he produced had not been specifically tailored for ethics. The ideas he echoed therein seem in tune with the views he expressed in his literary accomplishments on ethics. In *Cahiers pour une morale*, Sartre seems confident and resolute that there is a link between ontology and morality.

Chapter 4: Examining Sartrean Ethics

CHAPTER FIVE

Views against Sartrean Ethics

This chapter supports the notion that Sartre has relevance in ethics. It examines diverging viewpoints in the literature. The chapter focuses on the many points of view that tilt the debate against Sartre. The chapter explores hallmarks of the arguments that are often echoed against Sartre. It centers on three arguments: the publication argument, the substance argument, and the theoretical argument. The chapter argues in favor of an all-inclusive approach, which will help us grasp the crux of Sartrean ethics. The chapter further explains the reason an all-inclusive approach would make it possible to examine Sartrean ethics. It shows a difference between the works, which Sartre published himself and the ones, which Arlette Elkaim-Sartre, published on his behalf (for example, postmortem publications).

CHAPTER

5

A Household Name

Jean-Paul Sartre was a giant thinker in many literary disciplines. He was a household name in philosophy. As Sartre proved himself as a powerhouse in moral philosophy, he also became the target of constant scrutiny.

Philosophers within the rank of Jean-Paul Sartre are not always appreciated right off the bat. Their publications are often rebuked. Their magnum opus could be considered controversial, at least at first. Their creeds [or their credenda] could be rejected before any considerations had been offered to their intellectual relevance.

Chapter 5. A Household Name

Disagreements can go as far as expressing contempt for the compilations, which fall outside a certain model.

Sartrean ethics is being treated in a similar fashion. Yet, objections refuting Sartre's moral thoughts seem emanated from the thinking that his approach does not adhere to popular expectations. His views do not fall in line with what ethical writings should be. There is little sympathy for the Sartrean ethical model.

I do not mean to sound presumptuous. But my effort to show a positive imagery of Sartrean ethics is genuine. Critics are likely to approach the issue differently. I do not share their position.

We could not consider disagreements against a prominent thinker like Jean-Paul Sartre as something out of the ordinary. As John Anderson points out in the book titled *"Discourse on Thinking: A Translation of Gelassenheit,"* this is hardly a new idea in modern literature. He notes:

> *"There are many who resist a certain kind of philosophy. They find it hard to enjoy, abstract, and apparently of no great practical value. It seems to them vague and obscure nonsense. There have always been such people in the various epochs of human history, just as there have always been those who find the revelations of speculative thinking to be of utmost importance."*[1]

Paul Arthur Schilpp echoes a similar understanding. He argues that it is undisputable that different experts would find different ideas within the writings of the same philosopher.[2] It is not surprising that diverse critics approach the origin of Sartrean ethics from conflicting perspectives. People may hold different viewpoints about certain issues of interests.

Ethics is a topic of interest in various fields of study. I am not surprised of the degree of disunity that exists about the concept. I am not surprised that observers seek to weaken Sartre's literary relevance in ethics. The atmosphere that prevails toward Sartre's moral philosophy is barely a new approach.

Because of the many disagreements and misinterpretations about Sartre's published works, whom should we trust? The answer is not as clear-cut as one would want it to be. In the present work, brief though it is, I effort to examine, at least to the best of my intellectual fecundity[3] and writing abilities, the degree to which Sartre deserves a recognizable spot in the ethical discipline.

EXAMINING DIVERGING POSITIONS

Opinions conflict with the role Sartre played in ethics. People who hold a lesser esteem for Sartre or his philosophy reject any notion, which claims that he could be considered a moral philosopher. These pundits are convinced that Sartre contributed little, if anything at all, to this philosophical discipline.

I disagree with such views. Is there a possibility that anti-Sartrean positions might be founded? Let us explore the extent of those views.

There is not a big fissure *vis-à-vis* the philosophy of Jean-Paul Sartre and his views about ethics. This is the case despite the presumption that Sartre is irrelevant in ethics. When it comes to Sartre's moral thoughts, convictions are normally scattered on various perspectives.

Most pundits agree that Sartre is not a moral philosopher. There are also those who espouse a different perspective about the nature of Sartre's philosophical identity. Why is there such a rift in the debate? The answer may be found in the literature.

A different breed of observers nourishes a positive regard for Sartre's literary relevance in moral philosophy. They examine his approach to ethics under a more appreciative lens. I am more interested in such viewpoints.

What proof do I have to support the claim that Sartrean ethics exists beyond any doubt? How could I justify the notion that Sartre deserves any intellectual merit in ethics? The answer is simple. Sartre suggested such a link in many of his ideas about freedom.

Many opponents argue that Sartre does not deserve any place in the ethical domain. Other critics echo that parts of Sartre's publications could be considered as the pillars of his ethical concerns. I espouse the latter view.

The ethics, which Sartre expressed in his works, often becomes the subject of countless criticisms. Few literary publications could be used to support that ethics. But to reiterate, a few scholars espoused a neutral approach on the subject. Their insights are worth considering.

Thomas Anderson refutes the notion that Sartre did not outline his ethical viewpoints in his written works, notably in his posthumously released materials. The author also refutes that ethics, although he did so in part. In *Sartre's Two Ethics,* Anderson echoes that Sartrean ethics is not all that it could be. Elizabeth Bowman and Robert Stone highlight positive portions of Jean-Paul Sartre, notably the Sartrean approach to ethics. In *Sartre Alive,* they examine the different drawbacks of that ethics. I discuss these views in greater length in subsequent chapters (*see* Chapters 9, 10, 11, and 12).

Jean-Paul Sartre's legacy as a moral philosopher is uncertain. Critics even suggested that such a legacy has been tarnished beyond repair. Many scholars are relentless in their self-given duty to refute the ethical prowess of Jean-Paul Sartre, while recognizing him as a giant philosopher. This is absurd. Yet, there is no way to change that incongruent reality.

The literature is unforgiving, if not brutal, on this front. The current debate is laden with conflicting opinions against Sartre. It is unclear whether I could undo all that damage in this text alone. Nonetheless, I am motivated to engage this project to the best of my intellectual abilities. It makes sense to defend the Sartrean approach to moral philosophy. It is relevant to defend Jean-Paul Sartre as a moral philosopher.

POINTS OF CONFLICT

Three major points of dispute are often levied in the literature against Sartre. They are mutually exclusive. I outline them as follows: *The Publication Argument*, *The Substance Argument*, and *The Theoretical Argument* (*see* Figure 4.1). Let me explore them in a broader context. Let me introduce the gist of the views echoed in those arguments.

Sartre's approach to ethics is poorly explored, unexplored, or, without a hitch, unknown. My objective is to depict a different side of Jean-Paul Sartre's intimation with the topic. It is important to underline that Sartre played a significant role in ethics. He has an important intellectual relevance in the discipline.

There is a need to focus on the compilations logged by various experts, including opponents and admirers alike. There is a need to examine the essentiality of Sartre's approach to ethics through the lenses of various inquirers. There is a need to explore the types of criticisms echoed by prominent scholars. There is a need to refer to points noted by scholars in the field. There is a need to explore the views echoed by those who specialize in the theoretical principles, which Sartre made famous during his career.[4]

There is a need to refer to other *exposés* as well. There is a need to examine the views expressed by several authors and relevant contributors in human ontology. There is a need to examine the positions echoed by those who have developed an intimate understanding of Sartrean philosophy. There is a need to center on those who are familiar with Sartrean ethics.

The best way to examine disputes against Sartre is by dissecting the arguments that are often echoed against him. Critics have raised so many issues that it might be difficult to pinpoint the essence of the debate. Let us examine three types of criticisms (to learn more, *see* Figure 4.1). These points of strife seemed carefully designed to dismiss the scope of Sartrean ethics.

THE PUBLICATION ARGUMENT

The major point of dissension that is often resounded against Jean-Paul Sartre is the argument I coin: *The Publication Argument* (*see* Figure 4.1). This articulation illustrates the types of materials, which Sartre published, as opposed to the writings, which he produced, but never published himself. Excepting the book titled *Notebooks for an Ethics*, the known works credited to Sartre are not available to the public.

Critics have suggested the items Sartre published are trivial to the field of ethics. They inferred there is no tangible evidence to support the existence of a Sartrean ethics. Let us explore this argument in depth.

The publication argument is among the many refutations that have been raised to counter Sartrean ethics. The view is that Sartre was not prolific in ethics, at least when compared to other areas he explored during his career. There is a bit of truth to that assertion. But that is not [at least, self-evidently] the reason dissenting voices refuse to concede Sartre a role in this literary discipline.

Before we delve in criticisms, it is worth pointing out two sides to the issue. The first one echoes criticisms that center on the published materials. The argument is that such materials were not chiefly tailored for ethics. The second twist of this reasoning outlines the notion that Sartre's unpublished pamphlets are not worthy of any intellectual scrutiny. This is so even though they were intentionally framed for ethics. The reason often reiterated is that these manuals are incomplete; they are fragmented.

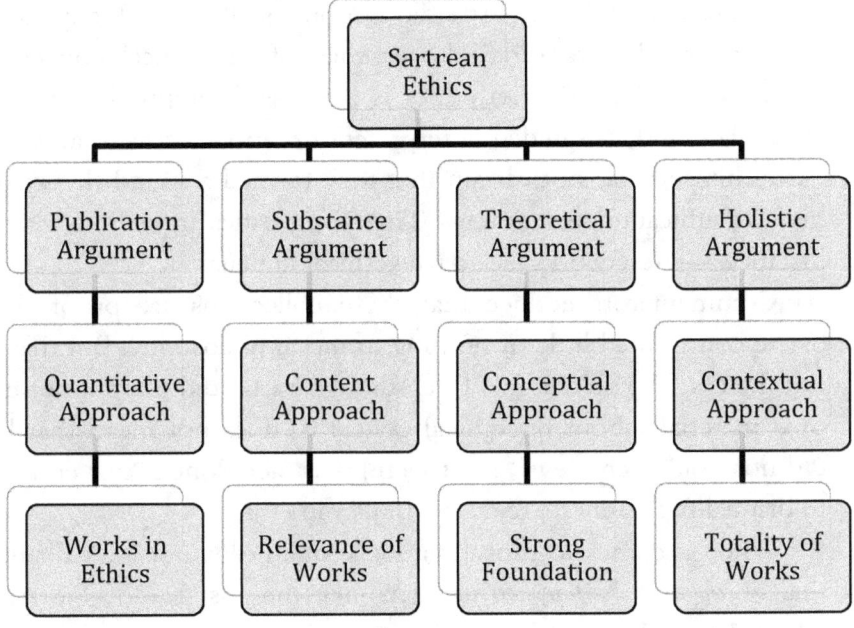

Figure 5. 1: Approaches to Sartrean Ethics

I have a different take about the recently released materials, which Sartre is said to have compiled about ethics. I would say that both published and unpublished items constitute Sartre's literary repertoire in ethics. Failing to examine these items (as a whole) would be shortsighted. These materials, I would echo, deserve more scrutiny than a superficial examination.

Chapter 5. A Household Name

Works Published Versus Works Produced

Sartre produced many materials related to ethics during his career. Such materials include several opuses (opi) and other manuscripts. As echoed here thus far, he published fewer of these essays himself.

Critics contend that Sartre did not personally publish any piece of literature that captured the essence of his ethical concerns. Critics argue that Sartrean ethics is baseless; it emphasizes vague inferences and misguided interpretations about ideas that even Sartre himself was not certain that they formed a sound theory of his own ethical understandings. Therefore, critics argue that—in all instances—these works lack a true ethical dimension.

Commentators adduce that these collections are proof that Sartre contributed little or nothing to moral philosophy. But this is not the case, I would argue. Even though Sartre did not put out his own materials about his ethical concerns, does not mean that he did not hold such views. As it were, that fact alone is not enough to disqualify Sartre as a relevant thinker in ethics.

When it comes to those materials, one needs not look further than *Being and Nothingness* to decipher the essence of Sartrean ethics. I would even contend that there is an ethics to be found in every facet of Sartre's approach to human ontology. A thorough reading of the noted publication would support that viewpoint.

Sartre is credited to have compiled several notes discussing the nature of his approach to ethics. Many of these ideas have been published in the *Notebooks for an Ethics*. Sartre also produced other travails in the domain. They include lectures and a few unfinished manuscripts, which were tailored for ethics (*see* Chapter 6).

We must wonder about the real reasons contentious attitudes about Sartrean ethics persist. Answers are not clear. But the reality is that a divergence exists in the arguments that are often echoed to oppose Sartrean ethics. Such discrepancies are seldom explored.

THE SUBSTANCE ARGUMENT

While Sartre's publications deserve a better scrutiny, critics are quick to claim that such releases lack any intellectual substance. The gist of the debate often centers on the whim that a Sartrean examination of ethical problems lacks substance. I refer to this approach as *The Substance Argument*.

Critics argue that Sartre cannot be raised to the prominence of a serious philosopher in ethics. The reason that they offer is that Sartrean writings lack any intellectual relevance. The arguments that Sartre echoed in these written materials, observers are convinced, are mostly rhetoric.[5]

The issues insinuated from this understanding presume that Sartrean ethics is incongruent, vague, and incomplete. Put another way, Sartre did not compile the necessary ideas for a sound ethical foundation. As we will uncover later, the refusal to admit Jean-Paul Sartre as a relevant thinker in the ethical domain emanated from misguided understanding about the compilations, which he produced and not congenitally, by its own nature, on the persuasive merit of those items. This is not even the case that critics are concerned with the intellectual worth of Sartre's main arguments.

There is a need to examine the extent to which analysts support the view that a Sartrean ethics exist. Even though observers are likely to accept that Sartre produced a large body of work in the domain, they also disagree with the quality of such titles. I elaborate on this portion of the debate later.

Chapter 5. A Household Name

My position is irrefutable; Sartrean ethics exists. I refute any viewpoint, which suggest the contrary. So far, I have echoed that understanding as cogently as possible. But there is more.

To say it again, the present work is not a fanatical defense of Jean-Paul Sartre. It is motivated by a desire to see a fair assessment of Sartrean ethics. Sadly, that degree of neutrality does not exist in the present literary discourse.

I would not argue that Sartre was a pioneer in the ethical discipline. His insights are of an utmost significance. Sartre deserves a more appreciative scrutiny in ethics.

I do not think that Sartre was a *guru* in the ethical domain. It could be difficult to make such a claim only by relying on the materials, which he produced while alive. I could not even make such a claim by relying on the materials, which Elkaïm-Sartre published on Sartre's behalf. Nevertheless, when considering both items that Sartre published himself and the materials released on his behalf, it might become evident that the Sartrean approach to ethics is worthy of a thorough examination.

Even though the posthumously released materials could be considered incomplete or disjointed, that does not make them less important. We could regard them as central points of reference for a serious debate. These materials could help us pinpoint the extent of Sartre's involvement in ethics. They might help us set the stage for a thorough scrutiny of Sartre's intellectual merit in the field.

The Theoretical Argument

Another view worth noting in the debate is the notion that Sartre's own assessment of his ethics is lacking a theoretical foundation. I refer to this approach as *The Theoretical Argument*. But this is a misguided slant to understanding the scope of Sartrean ethics.

The contention here is that Sartrean ethics is too simplistic. It is rudimentary. Thus, it is incompatible with the works, which Sartre compiled during his literary career. Even if that argument were true [or could be true], it would still be inadequate to undermine the value of the treaties, which Sartre produced about ethics.

The depth of Sartrean ethics is not that shallow. The important point to highlight in the literature is that little or nothing is known about that ethics. Of course, this is not because of Sartre's inability to outline his ideas coherently. Rather, it is because commentators often overlook the essence of the most valuable works, which Sartre produced about ethics.

Most of the arguments offered in opposition to Sartrean ethics reveal the extent of speculations about the nature of the collections of essays, which Sartre produced. Short from examining every angle of Sartre's role in moral philosophy, one could only speculate about his contributions to this discipline. Few inquirers have approached these works from a different perspective. That is why I am convinced that most criticisms about Sartre in the ethical domain are misguided.

The best way to examine the reach of Sartrean ethics is by espousing an *open-mind attitude*. But that open-mindedness must be ongoing, even during the reviewing process. Many inquirers have approached the issues from a narrow perspective. Critics claimed that they could not locate the fundamentals of Sartrean ethics. Is there any truth to that claim? It is [probably] not the case.

There is a need to explore the possible reasons analysts seem certain that Sartre played no role in ethics. Critics have charged that Sartrean ethics is, without any elaboration, not there. In my view, these analysts are in error. Perhaps they have been searching for Sartrean ethics in the wrong place. That ethics is not a mystery. It is located all over the place in Sartrean philosophy.

Chapter 5. A Household Name

There is ample evidence to offer a sound critique of the types of criticisms that are often levied *contra* Sartre. Dissenting views appear unjustifiable. Such criticisms seem emanated from mistaken assumptions about the man and his intellectual worth. It would be counterproductive to judge a philosopher only by the scope of his knowledge or by the extent of his analytical talents.

The focus of criticisms would be best served if they were directed toward examining the depth of Sartre's intellectual contribution in ethics. That way, they would serve a more fruitful purpose.[6] In recent years, Sartrean ethics has been relegated to the number of literary items, which he published. Critics focused on the essence of the materials, which had been published on his behalf.

Sartre's written works about ethics have been judged inadequate solely based on the breadth of the arguments, which Sartre proposed in these materials. Instead of having a great debate about the crux of Sartre's role in ethics, commentators often measure the extent of that role. By any measure, they are bogged down in the publication argument. They often ignore other pertinent factors.

Critics seldom consider that Sartre's way of examining ethics is an integral part of his philosophical brand. Sartre could not examine the individual in the ontological plane without considering the role of ethics. That ethics is everywhere. It is omnipresent within Sartrean philosophy. It is plain in his publications about existentialism. Such ethics could be made out by exploring the many works, which Sartre compiled during his literary career.

I recognize that the previous assertion could be considered a grandiose statement. It might be daft or even intellectually dishonest to suggest that everything that Sartre ever wrote is a part of his ethical project. To be clear, this is not what I am saying here.

If one were to search for Sartrean ethics in just one location (for example, in one set of documents), it might be complicated, if not impossible, to locate such ethics. To remediate this limit, I offer an all-inclusive approach. But what does the term all-inclusive mean in the present context? Let us explore this concept further.

THE HOLISTIC ARGUMENT

What would be an all-inclusive approach? What would be such an approach? I noted the need for an all-inclusive approach. This is the best way to place Sartrean ethics. I have not delved in the true meaning of the term here. Let us explore possible answers.

A *holistic approach* suggests inclusive modes of analysis. We must examine all facets of Sartrean ethics. We must do so not just for the literary pieces, which Sartre produced, but also for the materials, which Elkaïm-Sartre put out on her father's behalf posthumously. Such an approach is not another layer of sophistication; it is not another complication to decipher Sartrean ethics. This understanding could be considered a commonsensical approach to a simplistic problem.

Examining Sartrean ethics demands an inclusive perspective. It needs an *all-of-the-above* approach. But if we were to accept the assertion that morality is a human set up, it would make sense to examine the origin of morals through the agency of the individual who claims to hold such values.

It would make sense to examine every front of the being by looking into the way that the person frames [or rationalizes] his conducts. Sartrean philosophy offers such an insight into the being via phenomenological ontology. Why critics are likely to overlook this facet of the debate? I am not sure what to answer here.

An all-inclusive approach could be considered a simplistic way of examining Sartrean ethics. Critics might claim this is an exhibition of my limited capacity to grasp Sartre's take on ethics. I would not refute that view.

To echo a previous concession, I am not a Sartrean scholar. I do not base my analysis on years of researching the man. This work points out the speculative nature of this literary discipline. But my position, however mistaken it might be to some analysts, has an intellectual merit.

Despite the previous concessions, few people could refute the idea that an *all-inclusive approach* to examine the extent of Sartrean ethics would yield a better understanding of that ethics. Such an approach, in my view, would allow a better examination of the quality of the texts, which Sartre produced. Such an approach would also reveal the nature of the works, which clearly describe Sartre's ethical concerns.

I cannot fathom the reason critics would refute such a strategy to identify Sartrean ethics. I am confused about the reason most scholars subject that ethics to such a high standard. What sets the Sartrean model to ethics apart from other approaches? I am not sure.

Commentators often found it difficult, if not impossible, to afford Sartre any credit in ethics. They often found it hard to make out ethics from Sartre's literary imprints. But their frustration in not being able to locate the ethics that they expected suggests that they were optimistic in locating that ethics in the first place. They expected to locate Sartrean ethics, as if that ethics should have been obvious.

What is it about Sartrean ethics that makes it elusive or difficult to decipher? What is it that critics are seeking from Sartre's written works? How would we recognize the Sartrean model to ethics? Are there specific terms or terminologies, which Sartre should have used, but failed to use? Are there specific issues, which Sartre should have discussed, but failed to discuss? What is it that opponents object about when it comes to Sartre's examination of ethics? Once again, I am not sure what to say.

Putting the previous issues aside, we could examine a broader question. For instance, we could ask about the characteristics of ethics in the essays, which Sartre produced. But I am not sure how to approach such a question without considering the role of freedom in the way that the being makes out his world. I am unsure about the reason analysts assert that Sartre lacks any intellectual valor in ethics.

Critics might say that the previous viewpoint is a trivial way of approaching the issues. But Sartrean ethics, I would say, is not that complicated to decipher. I recognize that such an issue is not that simple. But there ought to be a balanced approach in the debate. This is the best way, I am certain, to determine the scope of Sartrean ethics.

Examining the term ethics demands an introspective approach. Any inquiry about the concept should examine the role of the individual in the community where he evolves. An inquirer should also examine the relation the being entertains with other members in the community.

When it comes to examining Sartrean ethics, that task should be easier. In the Sartrean world, for instance, the individual plays a major role in his own ethical situations. The being is at the center of Sartre's literary imprints. But what is missing from that ethical approach? Why commentators could not find an ethics in the documents, which Sartre produced, is beyond me.

To be unequivocal, I am not suggesting that Sartrean ethics is easy (or should be easy) to make out. But I would echo that ethics should not be that difficult to discover. There is an ethics to be found in every characteristic of Sartrean philosophy. An all-inclusive approach would reveal such an ethics. The reality is that inquirers have seldom approached Sartrean ethics from such a perspective. This is what I propose to do in the next few chapters.

Chapter Notes

[1] Heidegger, *Discourse on Thinking*, 11.

[2] Schilpp, *The Philosophy of Jean-Paul Sartre*.

[3] Guyau, *A Sketch of Morality Independent of Obligation Or Sanction*. This author refers to the term "Intellectual Fecundity" as a way to explain the tendency young men often experience to exhaust their lives by engaging in premature excess of intellectual labor. I use this term to denote that my understanding of Sartrean ethics and the literature might not be at the stage where writing a book would make sense. I wanted to dedicate my first work about philosophy to Jean-Paul Sartre.

[4] I am referring to Sartrean scholars.

[5] Bernstein, *Praxis and Action*.

[6] The point I am trying to articulate here is that, when the goal is to examine a philosopher objectively, the quantity of work produced should not matter. Rather, the focus should be on the quality of those works.

CHAPTER SIX

Works about Ethics

This chapter is relatively short. It discusses Sartre's major literary ideas about ethics. It examines the collections, which Sartre published about ethics during his legendary literary career. It also explores popular publications, such as *Being and Nothingness* and *Critique of Dialectical Reason*. The chapter examines the foundations of Sartrean ethics. It explores features of major concepts, including the notion of *"being and non-being."* This chapter further relays the publications, which Sartre released himself. These texts have an ethical facet, which pundits often overlook or undermine. The chapter stresses on the notion that Sartre developed a clear ethics in his many written works.

CHAPTER

6

SARTRE'S MAJOR WORKS

It is widely known that Jean-Paul Sartre published several books, some of which are popular. Sartre wrote on an array of subjects. He examined various topics. His major contributions to human literature came from two of his most acclaimed titles. They include, *Being and Nothingness*, which was originally published in 1943 and the *Critique of Dialectical Reason*, originally published in 1960.

In these two volumes, Sartre sketched out the theoretical scheme for the doctrine commonly known as *Existentialism*. He further refined this approach to human existence in other publications. In *Being and Nothingness,* for instance, Sartre explained

Chapter 6. Sartre's Major Works

what he meant by the notion of freedom. He did so with an outmost intellectual rigor.

Sartre discussed the extent of a human ontology in relations to the capacity of the individual to enjoy or reject this freedom. The noted book was not specifically designed to address Sartrean ethics in depth.[1] The manuscript includes several arguments, which also have ethical implications.

Sartre was a moralist in the true sense of the term. Even so, the Sartrean approach to ethics is not popular. It is not universally accepted. The common belief is that Sartre's works were not that developed. They were not well known or perhaps well understood to make it possible for others to consider Sartre a famous philosopher in ethics in the likes of Plato, Aristotle, Thomas Aquinas, Thomas Hobbes, John Locke, Emmanuel Kant, Frederick Nietzsche, Gabriel Marcel, John Stuart Mill, Jacques Maritain, and Augustine of Hippo, just to name a few.

Critics are unforgiving against Sartre. Deciphering a Sartrean imprint in ethics, they say, remains a far-fetched undertaken. The argument could be made that commentators are wrong. Deciphering Sartrean ethics is not such a chimerical project.

Most analysts are quick to dismiss Sartre as someone who has displayed an irrefutable ethical side in his essays. Criticisms have also come from those who have had a closer examination of Sartre's writings. David Pellauer, a person who translated Sartre's book *Cahiers pour une morale* (*Notebooks for an Ethics*) from French to English, has expressed little or no faith in Sartre as a moral philosopher. This is shocking.

Like Pellauer, Ruman Ji has also been excessively critical of Sartre's approach to ethical issues. Ji notes that Sartre could not honor his promise to devote his future literary projects to ethics.[2] Despite countless efforts, he never concretized his goals, Ji argues.[3] The scope of Sartre's examination of his ethical concerns is unclear.[4] From Ji's standpoint, Sartre convinced himself not to engage in this discipline.

The previous understandings, I would argue, fall within the scope of speculative statements about Sartre and his role in the ethical discipline. Sadly, that attitude plagues the current literary discourse. Even so, these views did not arise from on any truth. In truth, no one knows the reason Sartre abandoned his works about ethics.

The reality is that both Ji and Pellauer are not alone in their assessment of the reason (or the possible motives) that led Sartre to abandon his written works. The reason offered by most analysts, including Ji, is that Sartre discovered that his dialectical ethics was not developed fully, at least as he expected. Sartre could not produce a compelling ethical tableau about his philosophy.[5] Many scholars have abounded in the same logic. Many people consistently sought to deny Sartre a role in ethics.

What is the nature of criticisms against Sartre? I do not subscribe to the views expressed by most pundits. I believe Sartre played a major role in the ethical discipline. I have a few elements to support that argument. Let us examine the extent to which critics have underestimated Sartre's role in the ethical domain.

IMPORTANT WORKS ABOUT ETHICS

Jean-Paul Sartre produced various collections of essays, which directly (or indirectly) addressed his ethical concerns. Such works include: *Transcendence of the Ego* (1936) and *Notebooks for an Ethics* (1983). They are available in most libraries.

Sartrean ethics "is also concretely embodied in his lengthy study of Flaubert."[6] At the time Sartre died, these works were organized and were close to being published in their current forms.

Other compilations, however, were not well settled. They were unorganized. Many of these items were not ready for publication.

David Pellauer argues that *Notebooks for an Ethics* is a prelude to Sartrean ethical ideas. The text is only a preparation for an ethics, he echoes. According to Pellauer, the notebooks may only induce a thorough treatment of Sartre's writings about ethics.[7]

Despite translating Sartre's most pertinent texts about moral philosophy, Pellauer does not support the Sartrean approach to ethics. This is odd. Pellauer should have been a defender of Sartrean ethics. He is among the few scholars who have had the opportunity to decipher Sartre's major works in the field. Pellauer meticulously dissected Sartre's fundamental understandings about ethics.

Many observers could argue that this is precisely the reason Pellauer should enjoy a certain authority or some legitimacy in his scrutiny of Sartrean ethics. But to the contrary, I would retort. Pellauer's views about Sartrean ethics come across more like an interpretation of Sartre's ideas, rather than a translation of that.

His views (Pellauer) do not differ from the ones that are often typified in the literature. Most of Pellauer's arguments seem akin to the types of disparagements often echoed by those who seem lost in the translation between what Sartre is saying and what they grasp from those words. Now, I am not sure whether Pellauer's views came before the criticisms, which make up the current debate or whether they are the results of the debate itself.

Manifestly, not everyone shares Pellauer's viewpoints on this issue. Supporters of Sartrean ethics, for instance, point out that Sartre produced several materials, which are crucial in capturing his views about the subject. Critics marked that ethics has always been a part of Sartrean philosophy. Although the *Notebooks for an Ethics* had been published in the 1980s, Sartre, to reiterate, compiled these materials around the late 1940s (between 1946 and 1947).[8]

Therefore, it would not be exaggerated to say that Sartre had a long history in the field.

David Pellauer, however, refutes the previous claim. He notes that Sartre never published his own ideas about ethics during his lifetime.[9] Along similar views, observers have often wondered whether what is known about that ethics accurately reflects Sartre's true objects. This is a ridiculous argument, I would argue.

No doubt Sartre had developed a true ethics during his lifetime. Whether his approach was well developed enough at the time could be classified as a different question or such a discrepancy could be explored from a different angle. Such an approach could be explored from a different perspective. We could debate the nature of that ethics from a separate angle. We could assess the intellectual merit of the documents, which Sartre produced, qualitatively and not quantitatively.

Almost every piece of literature that sought to rebuke Sartre's role in ethics also relied on Sartre's own writings. Thomas Anderson, for instance, notes that what is known about Sartrean ethics comes from understandings about Sartre's early works. Even those who deny Sartrean ethics make that determination by considering Sartre's early compilations in the field.

We know now that ethics had mutated in several phases during Sartre's intellectual maturation. Thomas Anderson sought to prove a clear distinction between Sartre's first, second, and third ethics. From Anderson's viewpoint, when it comes to consistency and coherence, Sartre's early works do not provide a clear picture of his ethical concerns.

Anderson argues that Sartre's first ethics was feeble and intellectually shaky. This ethics was incomplete and disjointed. Most of the statements Sartre made in his previously published materials were scattered in the materials, which he produced in other areas.[10] This is perhaps the reason the foundation and the general structure of Sartrean ethics were not clear.[11]

Anderson insinuated that observers are misguided in their approach when they seek to examine Sartre's literary relevance in moral philosophy, for example when it comes to the recently minted materials. Anderson suggests that, while there are discrepancies about the number of compilations, which are available, a particular set of known materials, which Sartre purportedly produced for a lecture he provided in Rome in 1964, are more than plenty to help us distillate the nature [or the scope] of his ethical concerns. Anderson further notes that "Enough can be found in these resources to enable us to obtain a good deal of information about Sartre's second morality."[12]

It must be noted that few inquirers have conducted a detailed examination of the *Notebooks for an Ethics*.[13] This piece of literature, Anderson notes, provides a more coherent picture of Sartrean ethics. The recently released (posthumous) materials, coupled with a thorough examination of the notebooks, would afford us a better understanding of the approach Sartre adopted in his ethics. Such an approach, Anderson echoes, would "enable us to resolve the major issues that have arisen among critics concerning the nature and the contents of Sartre's early ethics."[14]

As well as the previously noted collections, Sartre produced other materials that were scrupulously tailored for ethics. Robert Stone and Elizabeth Bowman remarked the existence of several unpublished materials, which Sartre produced from either lectures he delivered in the past or lectures he intended to give in the future. These scholars are convinced that Sartre played a relevant role in the ethical discipline.

The newly uncovered materials, which Stone and Bowman are convinced, constitute the foundation of Sartre's position about ethics. There is enough information in Sartre's literary repertoire to suggest that he was active [regularly] in moral philosophy. The next part outlines a comprehensive recount of the literary items contained in Sartre's ethical catalog.

Unpublished Materials

Sartre compiled several materials, which distinctly decipher his intellectual outlook about ethics. Stone and Bowman, for instance, note that between November 1962 until the mid-1965, Sartre entrenched himself in "an extended writing project on morality and history."[15] They note that during that time, Sartre produced three writings about ethics. Most of these materials had not been published. "Only fragments of these works have thus far been released for public scrutiny," they also note.[16] Let us explore the scope of those materials.

Stone and Bowman note that Sartre produced several pages of typed materials about ethics (*see* Figure 6.1). It is believed that Sartre produced a plethora of handwritten materials as well. Anderson further notes that most of the materials Sartre wrote in preparation for a lecture in Rome were handwritten.[17] These materials are in the form of notes, which Sartre somehow wrote to himself.[18]

CHAPTER 6. SARTRE'S MAJOR WORKS

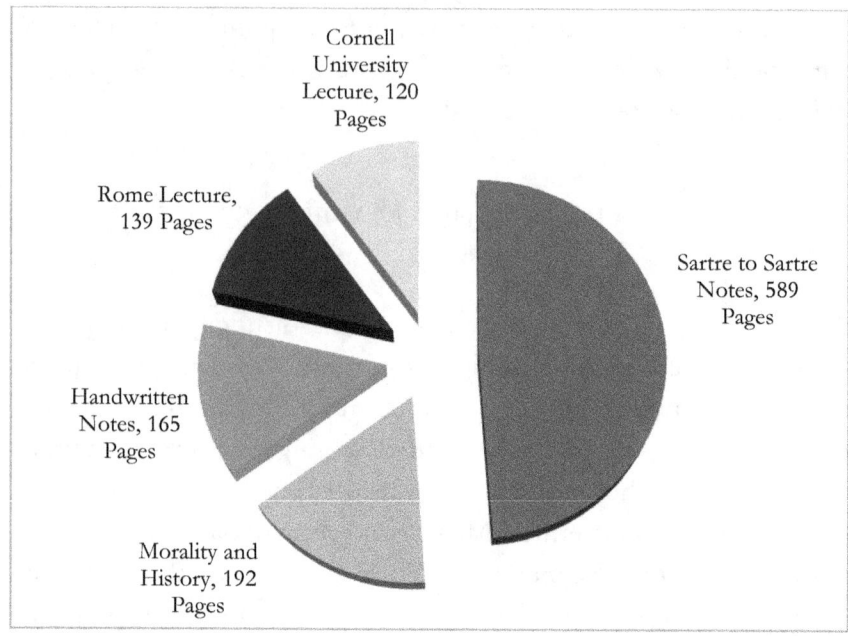

Figure 6. 1: Posthumously Released Works

The common reasoning is there could be more undisclosed materials out there about Sartre's moral thoughts. But the argument worth echoing is that Sartre was prolific in the field. This is so, even though he did not publish these works himself (*see* Figure 6.1 in the previous page; Source *Sartre Alive*, pp. 55-56).

The materials recently released by Elkaïm-Sartre largely include, but are not limited to, several manuscripts. Many of these materials include typed texts and handwritten documents. Parts of these materials are publication ready. Others are in bad shape; they may need extensive editing.

Posthumously Released Works

Roughly 165 handwritten pages	• No information available
Roughly 589 typed pages	• Mostly unorganized preparatory notes about ethics • From Sartre to Sartre
Roughly 139 typed pages	• Mostly organized notes for the 1964 Rome Lecture • These materials are close to publication form
Roughly 120 typed pages	• For the Cornell University Lecture • Morality and History • These materials are close to publication form
Roughly 192 typed pages	• Manuscripts • Morality and History

Many of these materials are notes, which Sartre wrote to himself. They include manuscripts, which Sartre prepared for lectures and other presentations. While compiling this work, I was under the impression that most of these items had not been released to the public.[19] But it is worth noting that, no matter what, this is an exhaustive repertoire about moral philosophy. The next portion of the manuscript features a sample of these items.

It is believed that Sartre prepared many of these materials listed above between 1964 and 1965, following a lecture he gave at the Gramsci Institute, in Rome. Sartre produced a typewritten manuscript, which contained around 499 pages of materials. This manuscript is believed to have existed since 1964 as well.

Sartre also produced another manuscript, which contained six completed sections. There are about 293 typewritten pages in that compilation (*see* Figure 6.1). This draft is believed to have resulted from a series of lectures, which Sartre was scheduled to deliver at Cornell University in 1965. Sartre canceled the lectures in protest of the American involvement in the Vietnam War. Therefore, Sartre could not deliver the lectures himself.

EXAMINING THE NOTEBOOKS

Critics often point out that both the recently uncovered manuscripts and most of already published materials are not succinct enough to depict a clear picture of Sartrean ethics. To sketch their views, they argue that many of the ideas contained in his notebooks are missing. These ideas do not lay out the foundation of an ethics.[20]

Critics argue that Sartrean ethics is scattered from many directions. To that extent, that ethics is inconceivable. It is disjointed; it is vague. I do not refute this assertion.

As noted in chapters 2 and 3, Sartre does not dispute the incongruity that characterizes his ideas about ethics. There is also the argument that Sartre's own approach to philosophy stemmed from his ethical notions, although his views are not stated in those terms. Let us revisit this part of the debate further.

Within the context of individual freedom, distinctly in his *Notebooks for an Ethics,* Sartre stressed on the need for the *"authentic"* subject to live without an ego.[21] This concept put the individual in contradiction with the self. The being is lost as he seeks to make a distinction between a self, which he may understand as genuine, and another self (his ego), which he may make out as subversive.

There is a clear ethical deviation in the Sartrean approach to freedom. There is a direct inference to ethics in the need for the individual to remain authentic. No doubt, a link between ethics and human ontology is plain in Sartrean philosophy. Let us explore this link deeper.

BEING AND NON-BEING

In earlier works, Sartre manifestly suggested that existentialism was born out of care for subjectivity. Broadly speaking, the individual could be understood as a split being. Thus, the individual could be assessed from two angles (see Chapter 8). He could be examined as two entities: a *"being"* and a *"non-being."*

A scrutiny of the individual's own approach to ethics is a precondition to understand the extent of Sartrean ethics. But such an approach, I would also highlight here, is supreme to support the views echoed in our analysis. Again, this view reinforces the notion that ethics is part of the ontological project itself.

Interpreting subjectivity, by contrast, seemed contrary to the presupposition, which Sartre eluded about a common or a social ontology. The individual is entrenched on a path toward an eternal conflict with the self, as he seeks to house his subjectivity in the world around him. I discuss this side of Sartrean ethics in Chapter 10.

As I have echoed in this work thus far, Sartrean ethics is harshly criticized. Without regards to the previously mentioned works, observers disagree that Sartre had developed an ethics worthy of consideration. To echo David Pellauer, there is no direct relation between ontology and ethics. Existence precedes ethics, Pellauer retorted.

Pellauer further projected the existence of speculations and controversies surrounding the extent of a Sartrean ethics. But his arguments debate whether both published and unpublished materials are relevant enough or are worthy of any intellectual curiosity.[22] I fervently reject this is position.

As discussed before, Sartrean philosophy is deeply intertwined with ethics. The believed abstraction of freedom itself makes no sense without grasping the role of ethics. When commentators refuse to admit that Sartre had an ethical part in his writings, they do not always depict the essence of their complaints. Their refutation of Sartrean ethics is not always clear. I am lost in the debate.

The current debate about the scope of Sartrean ethics is akin to a self-fulfilling prophecy. Sartrean ethics is considered irrelevant because observers say that it is so. But there is no tangible proof, which could demonstrate [without a shred of a doubt] that the Sartrean approach to philosophy in general (or his approach to ethics, for that matter) is irrelevant [or could be that way] in any way, shape, or form.

Despite views to the contrary, we must recognize that Sartre played a prominent role in proving himself as a moral philosopher. His literary contributions and his legacy in this domain are irrefutable. Excluding, pundits do not always see the issues from such a prism. What might explain their reservations *vis-à-vis* Sartrean ethics.

The Sartrean contribution to ethics is undeniable. It is irrefutable that Sartre published several written works, which are inextricably tied with ethics. Denying the extent of that reality is an error.

To support the previous assertion, we could look at Sartre's signature works. We could explore his theory about the nature of human existence. Let us explore the scope of the Sartrean approach to morality. Let us assess the nature of human ontology as well.

Chapter Notes

[1] I refer specifically to the book titled *"Being and Nothingness."*

[2] Ruman Ji, "Freedom: The Unifying Thread of Sartre's Ethics" (DePaul University, 1998).

[3] Ibid.

[4] Ibid.

[5] Ibid.

[6] Anderson, *Sartre's Two Ethics*, 2.

[7] Sartre, Notebooks for an Ethics.

[8] Lawrence C. Becker and Charlotte B. Becker, *Encyclopedia of Ethics* (Routledge, 2013).

[9] Sartre, Notebooks for an Ethics.

[10] Anderson, *Sartre's Two Ethics*.

[11] Ibid.

[12] Ibid., 2.

[13] Anderson, *Sartre's Two Ethics*.

[14] Ibid., 2.

[15] Stone and Bowman, "Sartre's Morality and History: A First Look at the Notes for the Unpublished 1965 Cornell Lectures," 55.

[16] Ibid.

[17] Anderson, *Sartre's Two Ethics*.

[18] Stone and Bowman, "Sartre's Morality and History: A First Look at the Notes for the Unpublished 1965 Cornell Lectures."

[19] This is the case only to my knowledge, of course.

[20] Ji, "Freedom."

[21] Flynn, "Jean-Paul Sartre."

[22] Sartre, Notebooks for an Ethics.

CHAPTER SEVEN

Defending Sartre

This chapter outlines the arguments that are often echoed in support of Sartrean ethics. It notes that Sartre always linked ethics to ontology. The chapter echoes that Sartre offered sound arguments to support his views on certain ethical issues, notably when it comes to the notion of freedom. The chapter highlights that Sartre laid down the foundation of his moral philosophy. It notes how Sartre describes the role of the authentic individual in forging his view about human conducts. The chapter explores the degree to which the individual invents his own values vis-à-vis his duties to the self. It examines the degree to which the individual invents his duties toward the community where he evolves.

CHAPTER

7

THE SCOPE OF SARTREAN ETHICS

Is there a reliable technique to examine the span of Sartrean ethics without appealing to the ideas that Sartre intimated in phenomenology? Is it possible to shed light on the extent of Sartre's moral philosophy, at least as a stand-alone field of study? For most critics, answers are in the negative.

Most observers rebuke Jean-Paul Sartre on the suspicion that little is known about his approach to ethics. But it is premature to dismiss the Sartrean ethical model on this ground alone. Sadly, this is the trademark of the current literary discourse.

Chapter 7: The Scope Of Sartrean Ethics

Sartre's unpublished materials in ethics are contentious. Even the published works are rebuffed without mercy. But it seems like there a little *ill will* toward the writings, which Sartre compiled about ethics.

Approaching the issues that way could lead to untrue assumptions about Sartre's true contribution to ethics. Denying Jean-Paul Sartre a role in ethics could impact his literary legacy negatively. The gist of the debate comes from poorly construed speculations about Sartre. They reflect a stubborn refusal to accept Sartre's intellectual merit.

There is no need to condemn Sartre. There is no need to lessen his approach to ethics. Critics could only speculate about the degree to which Sartre sought to prove a definitive intellectual footing in this area of philosophy. Sartre may have built his approach to ethics, perhaps unintentionally, as he tried to solidify his views about human ontology. But it is probable that his ethical concerns led to a better assessment of the being in the ontological plane.

In the Sartrean world, it is likely that ethics precedes existence. This is the case, notably when it comes to the notion of freedom. This is the case, even contrary to David Pellauer's viewpoints.

The ramifications, which underlie human connections, could also help explicate the essence of Sartrean ethics. But critics are likely to refute Sartrean ethics considering a relational recognition.[1] From this ideal, a Sartrean approach to human ontology is not a final accounting of human possibilities.[2] I agree with that viewpoint.

The Individual and the Community

There is a clear distention between the way the individual affects the community and the role of the community in defining the individual. The being recognizes the needs of the community may supersede his personal needs. The individual also accepts that he is part of a community. As he senses the *"other,"* he is sensed by the *"other"* as well.

The individual understands that he has a responsibility toward both the other and the community. That is the reason it is of a need to examine the Sartrean approach of certain ethical issues. But we must do so by referencing the previously stated relationship. Critics are skeptical about the nature of that relationship.

Many commentators adopted a firm approach about the extent to which a Sartrean ethics is even feasible. David Pellauer argues that anyone who ventures far enough to consider Sartre an expert in ethics must accept the possibility of being proved mistaken.[3] Pellauer's argument implies that, until we have had the opportunity to review all the materials or the writings Sartre produced about ethics, it would be best to presume that Sartre is not a philosopher in ethics.[4] I am flabbergasted by that assertion.

Pellauer's position is hypocritical. He prefers to deny the existence of Sartrean ethics, while accepting that such an ethics is incomplete. But Pellauer could not have it both ways. Either it is the case that Sartrean ethics exists (but it is also incomplete) or it does not exist at all.

I must echo that Pellauer is not alone in his assessment of Sartrean ethics. Various observers have engaged in a similar intellectual blunder. But the crux of the debate centers on the notion that Sartrean ethics is elusive.

Chapter 7: The Scope Of Sartrean Ethics

There is the view that Sartrean ethics is incomplete. But where is Sartrean ethics located exactly? I am not sure. The literature provides little or no hint on the matter.

Pellauer suggests that in our search to disentangle the nature of Sartrean ethics, we should leave no unanswered question. We should look at every possible angle to locate that ethics. Yet, Pellauer also suggests that within the materials he already consulted, there is no ethics to be found. Once more, I am shocked.

According to Pellauer, the ambiguity that overshadows the likelihood for a sound Sartrean ethics emanated from Sartre. Sartre did not have a good view of his own ethics, Pellauer contends. But this is not the case, I would echo.

It could be argued that Pellauer's rebuttal of Sartrean ethics is a needless poke at Sartre's intellectual relevance in ethics. I am not sure that Pellauer himself sought to attack Sartre directly or else. His stance undermines Sartre not to mention his legacy as a moral philosopher. This is a legacy, some might say, that is already shaken.

Pellauer's refusal of Sartrean ethics could not deny the existence of that ethics. Sartre had a clear roadmap for his ethics. The only problem is that Sartre never fully concretized his objectives, at least to his satisfaction. But that reality, in and of itself, does not minimize the value of his works.

Other analysts contend that Sartre failed to present his ideas about ethics convincingly. Pellauer, once more, argues that Sartre never outlined a clear mastery of his moral views. In Sartre's writings, there is no clear mention of *deontology* versus *consequentialism*, Pellauer retorted. Pellauer echoes that Sartre made no efforts to accept a metaethical reflection as being distinct from normative ethics.[5] From Pellauer's perspective, the existence of Sartrean ethics could be considered dubious, if not unlikely.

From a different perspective, Sartre did suggest his approaches to ethics in a clear format. But that ethics, I would argue, is plain to see in the existentialist paradigm. The Sartrean approach to human ontology could not be appreciated without grasping his views about ethics. Case in point, Sartre outlined many undeniable ethical ramifications in human conducts. I understand that it could be difficult to convince those who have a predetermined mindset about Sartre's capacity to produce a genuine ethics that he, in fact, played a role in the discipline.

Even if we were to contend that examining the human ontology, as a separate approach of an ethics, was outwardly the goal Sartre sought to carry out in his writings, critics might still say that such an examination was not essential. But my analysis does not aim at convincing unbelievers that Sartre developed relevant ideas in the ethical realm.

Various points about the ideas that Sartre reflected in his ideas about existentialism could frame the groundwork of his ethics. Whether Sartre developed a sound foundation or a well-developed enough approach to ethics is another question, which is not part of my concerns at this point. We could examine this question in a different project. Even so, I must point out that it would be imprudent to claim that Sartre did not present a roadmap, at least some seminal ideas, for a convincing ethics.

DENYING SARTREAN ETHICS

Finding out whether Sartre had developed a sound ethical foundation in his written works is a valid inquiry. It is not fair to bankrupt Sartrean philosophy, at the same time reducing Jean-Paul Sartre to a philosophical misnomer. It is not fair to degrade Sartre's intellectual worth just because pundits disagree with the views he voiced in his texts about moral philosophy.

This is where I take issues with criticisms. Sartre did offer relevant pointers about his ethics. He spelled out his stance on the subject coherently.

In his many works, Sartre hinted an individual's responsibility in human ontology. That responsibility had ethical ramifications. Even so, misjudgments about Sartrean ethics persist. The question is why that is the case.

There is a widespread misunderstanding about Sartre's frame of mind about the notion of human freedom.[6] A common deduction is that Sartre approached individual freedom from several angles. Sartre sought to distinguish important element between several sides of freedom.[7] One key distinction often echoed is that individual freedom is subjective. According to Sartre, the individual is always in charge of his freedom.

Sartre outlined this important individual responsibility in several of his post-war texts, including his publications on anti-Semitism (*Anti-Semite and Jew: An exploration of the etiology of hate*).[8] This depiction of an individual responsibility is also obvious in his writings about literature, including in *What Is Literature?*[9] Sartre notes the individual is free to choose his own path. But he must be aware of that likelihood.

In *Anti-Semite and Jew,* a book, which Sartre published in 1946, he explored freedom as it applies to *inauthenticity* and *authenticity*. In this famous book, Sartre sought to prove the role of individual freedom in human authenticity or the lack of that.[10] Therefore, authenticity is deeply set in Sartrean ethics or *existentialist* ethics.[11] Sartre argues that there ought to be a genuine effort by the individual to capture his freedom.

Sartre echoed a similar approach to individual responsibility in many of his magisterial works, for example in the book titled

Notebooks for an Ethics.[12] It is worth pointing out that the collections of essays, which Sartre produced express his tendency to place ethical concerns side-by-side with the way the individual conducts the self. While these works show that Sartre's ethical tableau was embryonic, they also project the undeniable, yet defensible, view of the duties of the individual to others.[13]

Sartre undividedly disclosed, in the most logical way, important notions about individual duties. He did so by explaining the being's duty or his moral responsibilities in the environment where he evolves. In pointing that out, I must echo that a Sartrean approach to such duties might not be understood as Kantian duties.[14] But it would be unwise to deny their ethical ramifications.

Constituents of the Sartrean views about individual duties could be best approached from a Hegelian lens. This view treats individual duties as a mutual recognition of moral responsibilities within the environment.[15] Denying a Sartrean role in ethics is like denying the obvious without any justification. Let us explore this idea further.

AUTHENTIC INDIVIDUAL AND ETHICS

When Sartre speaks of an individual duty, he reveals a clear representation of his ethical viewpoints. The possibility of an emerging portrait of Sartrean ethics offers a strong reply to those who suggest that Sartrean philosophy, ostensibly his approach to moral philosophy, is too liberal. A free individual answer to no one. He obeys few rules or norms within his environment.

The idea, which commentators often postulate, is that individuals are free to provide a license to vicious lifestyles, including other egocentric conducts, like serial killing.[16] A Sartrean approach to ethics suggests that freedom come from individual responsibility. But this approach refutes the previously stated argument. Individuals are free to be as they see fit. The individual still enjoys a moral duty to others.

Authentic individuals are aware of their environment to a point where they act in ways that promote positive connections. As well as acting with clarity and responsibility, existentially authentic individuals must respect others.[17] The individual is bound by certain moral principles, which guide his conducts in the world.

The way Sartre approaches ethics cannot be refuted based chiefly on impulsive reasons. Yes, Sartrean ethics is not fully developed. But this reality might be irrelevant, in this case, when it comes to finding out the intellectual merit of the arguments in that ethics. Any refusal of Sartre's role in ethics must eventuate from the intellectual merit of the materials, which he contributed to the discipline.

Any wisdom in arguments against Sartrean ethics must stem from the substantive nature of the ideas Sartre outlined in his collections of documents. Anything less than that would lead to inaccurate assumptions about the man and his overall contribution to the ethical discipline. I reject such an approach.

We should not rebuke Sartrean ethics simply because the arguments Sartre offered in supports of his views appear disjointed. It would be proper, as avid opponents of that ethics, to point out the flaws in logic. Criticism would make more sense if they were dedicated to pointing out the inaccurate arguments within the ideas Sartre proposed in his works. In my view, this is the essence of a true literary debate.

Sartre offered the necessary arguments to support the considerations that he developed a true ethics in his essays. I do not understand the reason his views invoke disputes. I do not grasp why his literary accomplishments in the field evoke passionate debates. The nature of his arguments does not invite staunch criticisms. It is not fair to subject Sartre, not to mention his works, to such claims, notably when such stands reveal misguided presumptions.

To say it again, a genuine Sartrean approach to ethics exists. Of course, whether such an approach also involves a genuine awareness to human ontology is not clear. Within that context, let us examine the issues further.

The next few chapters delve in the crux of Sartrean ethics. The goal is to decipher the preeminence of a human ontology in the Sartrean approach to ethics. These chapters highlight an irrefutable link between Sartrean philosophy and his approach to ethics. They lay out the foundation for a comprehensive assessment of Sartrean ethics.

Chapter Notes

[1] T. Storm Heter, "Authenticity and Others: Sartre's Ethics of Recognition," Sartre Studies International: An Interdisciplinary Journal of Existentialism and Contemporary Culture 12, no. 2 (2006): 17.

[2] Becker and Becker, *Encyclopedia of Ethics*.

[3] Sartre, Notebooks for an Ethics.

[4] Ibid.; Ji, "Freedom."

[5] Sartre, Notebooks for an Ethics.

[6] Detmer, "Freedom as a Value."

[7] Ibid.

[8] Jean-Paul Sartre, *Anti-Semite and Jew: An Exploration of the Etiology of Hate*, trans. George J. Becker (New York: Schocken, 1995).

[9] Jean-Paul Sartre and Steven Ungar, *"What Is Literature?" And Other Essays*, Third Printing edition (Cambridge, Mass: Harvard University Press, 1988).

[10] Becker and Becker, *Encyclopedia of Ethics*.

[11] Anderson, "Beyond Sartre's Ethics of Authenticity."
[12] Sartre, Notebooks for an Ethics.
[13] Heter, "Authenticity and Others."
[14] Ibid.
[15] Ibid.
[16] Ibid.
[17] Ibid.

CHAPTER EIGHT

Why Does Sartrean Ethics Matter?

This chapter explains the reason a methodical evaluation of Sartrean ethics is important. It echoes the role of self-identity in forging the Sartrean ethical concerns. The chapter examines how the individual could strive to proclaim his freedom from the world. The main idea here is that the individual finds himself in a constant struggle to assert his identity. Only in doing so, he might find freedom. The individual must consider the role of the community in creating the conditions that are necessary to gain [or even to lose] his freedom.

CHAPTER

8

UNDERSTANDING SARTREAN ETHICS

Critics are skeptical about the applicability of Sartrean ethics. But an important question worth asking is why we should be concerned about that ethics. To give an example, we must explore the reason the way Sartre approached ethical issues should matter.

A likely answer to consider is that ethics is the foundation of Sartrean philosophy. As noted as meticulously as possible in previous chapters, every feature of individual connections with others (or even the self) has ethical ramifications. Nonetheless, few critics are convinced this is the case; at least, in all instances.

Chapter 8: Understanding Sartrean Ethics

Critics argue that even Sartre did not grasp the potential role of ethics in his works. The argument often echoed is that there is no such a reality as a Sartrean ethics. Ji Ruman, for instance, asked whether there exists a real ethics in the writings of Jean-Paul Sartre, which might be worthy of a thorough examination.[1]

At first sight, a response to this question is not clear. But on further analysis, it becomes clear that the question itself came about because of an inaccurate assumption. The supposition is that Sartre failed to adhere to a particular set of ideals in his works. There is a lack of a clear scheme in his ethical approach.

Ji argued that it would be important to know whether a Sartrean ethics is even possible. If we were to examine Sartre's literary accomplishments, would we find an ethics, which Ji's argument presumes? The answer to Ji's question would be hard to settle. Suggesting an answer to Ji's question would invite false assumptions about Sartrean philosophy. I do not take that route. Sartre's publications deserve more than that.

It is not right to dismiss Sartre's literary accomplishments indiscriminately. We must not do so on the presumption that they were not methodically tailored for ethics. In chapter 6, I argued that Sartre produced a notable body of works, which are relevant to ethics. But this is a fact that most critics have recognized, including Ji.[2]

It might be necessary to reiterate that Sartre laid down the foundation for a sound ethical part in his literary portfolio. Sartre also developed a genuine approach to examining ethical problems. He did so rather expressively during his literary career.

There is an intrinsic link between freedom and ethics. Freedom is, as expressed in existentialism, the consequences of ideas connoted in *Being and Nothingness*. Such a notion plays a major role in bringing about Sartre's ethical concerns. For instance, Sartre defines freedom as the being of the *"for-itself."* He argues the being (the individual) is condemned to be free.

Sartre argues that gaining or enjoying freedom is not automatic. The individual must strive for that freedom. He must forever make the choice toward freedom. The individual must constantly seek freedom, which he might have carried out through the *"in-itself."*

In the concrete relations with others, Sartre hinges on the idea that the search for individual freedom is intertwined with how others make out the individual. The nature of human relationships can be complicated, at least within the scope of being subjected to an objectification by others. In *Being and Nothingness*, Sartre writes:

> *"We are now in a position to make explicit the profound meaning of desire. In the primordial reaction to the Other's look, I constitute myself as a look. But if I look at his look to defend myself against the Other's freedom and to transcend it as freedom, then both the freedom and the look of the other collapse. I see eyes; I see a being-in-the-midst-of-the-world. Henceforth the Other escapes me. I should like to act upon his freedom, to appropriate it, or at least, to make the Other's freedom recognize my freedom. But this freedom is death; it is no longer absolutely in the world in which I encounter the Other-as-object, for his characteristic is to be transcendent to the world."*[3]

A Long Search for Identity

Sartre notes that the individual is embarked in a constant struggle to proclaim his identity. By it, he is striving to gain his freedom from the subjectivity of others. The individual is entangled in facticity, whereby his freedom is determined by others. These are two different approaches to freedom, I would echo.

Chapter 8: Understanding Sartrean Ethics

The freedom Sartre speaks about in *Being and Nothingness* reflects the individual's intrinsic need (or the want) to be free. But with ethics, the types of freedom Sartre points out in his major literary achievements hinge a *co-dependency* between the individual and the world around him. Society plays a greater role in how individual freedom can be realized and gained.

The Sartrean approach to ethics centers on the view of a mutual recognition between *subjectivity* and *objectivity*. Understanding Sartre's ethical ideas is important. The previous illustration suggests that the individual is bound by certain values, which he cannot burst out from, to proclaim his freedom.

These ideas set the stage for a better appreciation of Sartre's outlook about human existence. Although Sartre's early works were not that concerned with societal issues, later in his career, Sartre had a different perspective. He began to deepen his views about the agency of social constraints, which for a better or worse, could affect individual freedom and, without omission, ethics.

Many commentators, notably Ji Ruman, argued that Sartre was caught in a bind.[4] Sartre could not carry out what he had set out to do, Ji echoed. Critics are also convinced that Sartre failed to come up with any compelling argument to solidify his ethics.

The popular presumption is that Sartre's ethical goals were frustrated; they were unattainable, critics echoed. But Sartre could never make up ideas, which he evoked in socialism, with his theory about freedom.[5] My understanding, on the other hand, is that the previous viewpoints are misguided.

There is an irrefutable link between freedom and morality. Denying that reality would not undermine such a link. Let us explore that link in more detail to clarify what I mean here.

The Link Between Freedom and Ethics

Sartre is a philosopher of conscience. His approach to ethics highlights subjective assessments, which the individual attaches to his reality. Let us analyze the *Being and Nothingness* and the effects of freedom on the being itself.

Sartre contends that the individual is always aware of the *"self."* To be a *"self,"* means to be with the self, he echoes. Sartre distinguishes between subjectivity (*For-itself*) and objectivity (*In-itself*). Sartre argues that these are two distinct modalities of being.

The *"being-for-itself"* is the decompression of being. Simultaneously, the *"being-in-itself"* is *"being an object."* The modality of being is an object. A *lack* will lead to the *want* to *act*.[6] This want, however, is guided by values, which is in turn informed by *"self-identity"* and the meaning that the individual attached to that *"self-identity."*

Sartrean ethics suggests that the lack of identity is precisely what freedom entails. Every individual has a natural want to be. Therefore, the being needs the capacity or the power to settle one's destiny in nature.

This want, as Sartre points out, is a failure. There are no possible ways out of this dead end. People are fundamentally defined in their being. Sartre talks about the objectification of the self. He notes that both *"being"* and *"non-being"* are opposite. They are contradictory.

Sartre also pondered on social ontology or a common ontology in human conducts. He argues, "Man is immersed in the historical situation."[7] The individual is constrained by his failure to understand the political organization or certain economic factors that determined his existence.

Sartre further notes the existence of others plays an important role in how the individual makes out his freedom and, inextricably, the freedom of others. In *Being and Nothingness*, Sartre talks about the effects of the existence of others through the look. In the noted book, Sartre writes:

> *"The other is presence for me to a 'being-in-a-pair-with-the-other.'"*[8]

Nonetheless, there is more to the notion of "The Other." Let us explore it further.

PERCEPTION OF "THE OTHER"

Sartre suggests that the other is important to the individual. This view allows the individual to appreciate the *"object-ness"* of the other. It also provides a real meaning for the individual to understand his relationship with the world, at first, in his *"being-for-others."*

The subject is not aware of the self. But he is aware of the object. The subject is the one who gives value to his world, through the object. Sartre precludes that *"subject-to-subject"* relationships are unidirectional. About social ontology, Sartre notes, individual groups or entities make out their relationship with other groups or entities within the context of *"Us"* and *"We."*

The precognition of *"Us"* is sensed as a real objective experience of a common object. The *"We"* is experienced by a particular consciousness.[9] Individual lives can be shared because of something subjective.

Sartre notes that there is no *"Us"* without a *"Them."* He also notes an everlasting conflict between being subject to the other's freedom and the individual's want or try to remove himself from that state of *object-ness*. This situation leads to feelings of hate, which can reveal itself through an avid want to see the death of the other. Sartre notes: "The one who hates projects no longer being an object; hate presents itself as an absolute positing of the freedom of the for-itself before the Other."[10]

Sartre further notes, "The being-for-other precedes and founds the being-with-others. Or else, there is not only a *"We-as-object,"* there is also a *"We-as-subject."*[11] The *"Us"* is understood as a real experience, which reinforces the individual view of the world in which he interacts. The *"Us"* that Sartre evokes here refers to an experience of *being-objects* in common.[12]

THE ONTOLOGICAL EXPERIENCE

Sartre points out in his writings that there is an ontological experience for the *"We."* The individual exists as *"Us"* only in the eyes of others.[13] The humanistic project of *"Us"* or the *"We"* as an object is a chimerical effort. It is the product of individual consciousness as an ideal impossible to arrive at.[14]

Sartre notes that from a Marxist perspective, the *subject of subjective* is a group. Sartre distinguishes between *"common actions"* vs. *"common thinking."* He argues that common thinking could lead to a build-up of the power necessary to change society. Common objectivity, on the other hand, could be the basis for oppression. The individual experiences subjectivity when he makes out himself as being objectified.

Sartre further notes that a fundamental piece about the pursuit of being is the individual wants to learn about others.[15] He wants to discover empirical data on them.[16] But the individual does not want to admit that subjectivity. In bad faith, the individual is constantly trying to catch up with himself. He falls in facticity, vulnerability, and finitude.

Sartre believes that the individual enjoys freedom at all time. For example, he enjoys such freedom when he evolves within a group or a social setting. Choice is the deliberation of our being, Sartre argues. This understanding infers that we choose the way of being in the world.

The previous depiction about freedom also suggests that despite the effects of the *"Others"* onto the individual, he remains in control of his world. This view highlights an important contradiction. Therefore, the individual is both free as *a unit* and as *a group*. It could be difficult to ignore the effects of ethics in both the actions of the individual and the influence of the community where he evolves.

Chapter Notes

[1] Ji, "Freedom."

[2] Ibid.

[3] Sartre, Being and Nothingness, 510–511.

[4] Ji, "Freedom."

[5] Ibid.

[6] Anderson, Sartre's Two Ethics.

[7] Sartre, Being and Nothingness, 561.

[8] Ibid., 340.

[9] Ibid., 536.

[10] Ibid., 532.

[11] Ibid., 537.

[12] Sartre, Being and Nothingness.

[13] Ibid., 547.

[14] Sartre, Being and Nothingness.

[15] Ibid., 781.

[16] Ibid., 781.

Chapter Nine

Different Approaches

This chapter explores the extent of different approaches that question the *quiddity* of Sartrean ethics. It elaborates on the ideas evoked by three scholars. They include Thomas Anderson, Robert (Bob) Stone, and Elizabeth Bowman. This chapter notes that Sartrean ethics exists, although it is embryonic or fragmented. It points out that the Sartrean approach to moral philosophy is incongruent. But only via an all-inclusive lens could we grasp the extent of that ethics. This chapter examines the viewpoints echoed by the noted scholars. It recounts the charges often evoked both for and against Sartrean ethics. The chapter further marks both positive and negative sides of the Sartrean ethical model. The arguments presented in the chapter refute the notion that Sartre does not have any relevance in this branch of philosophy. The views echoed center on an examination of Sartre's early ethics. The chapter revisits arguments in support of Sartrean ethics.

CHAPTER 9

A NEED TO GIVE SARTRE CREDIT

Despite criticism, Sartre has written a lot about ethics. But not much is known about that ethics. A recurrent question is why there is a gap in the literature about Sartre written works and what is known about them?

A logical answer to consider here is that there is a disinclination to give Sartre the proper credits for his literary materials about ethics. Sartrean ethics is not that disjointed, vague, and tangled. Rather, critics are reluctant to admit that Sartre has intellectual merits in the ethical discipline. Criticisms against Sartre are not unanimous.

Chapter 9: A Need To Give Sartre Credit

There are those who are softhearted in their disapproval of Sartre. In this case, I am referring to scholars who espouse a more neutral view about Sartrean ethics. They include, but are not limited to, Thomas Anderson, Elizabeth Bowman, and Robert Stone. Many of these experts reject the idea that Sartre had no bearing in ethics. But they espouse a more diplomatic approach in their examination of Sartre's literary accomplishments in the ethical domain.

Although commentators have argued that Sartrean ethics is an elusive notion and even Sartre himself did not often boast his understandings about the subject, scholars as those mentioned above, have examined constituents of Sartre's writings, which are relevant to ethics. A Sartrean examination of ethics is not elusive, these observers say. There is an ethics to be found in every portion of Sartre's materials, they echo.

Why should we take these scholars' views seriously? They are experts in the field. They are also familiar with the materials Sartre produced. These scholars seem more receptive to the idea that Sartre's ideas about ethics have intellectual merits, although with measured reservations. Many of these experts contended there is an irrefutable ethical side to Jean-Paul Sartre's philosophical identity. Since this ethics seems incomplete or ambiguous, there is a need for a thorough scrutiny of Sartre's postmortem written items to support that understanding.

It is true that many of the works that these scholars reviewed have not been published through ordinary channels. Other than the *Notebooks for an Ethics,* fewer (not official) publications have specifically detailed the nature of Sartrean ethics. Few existing materials directly numbered the reason Sartre abandoned his literary achievements in the field.

Many of such materials are also incomplete. But that does not deny that Sartre compiled these essays in the hope of widening his understanding of the being, mainly on the ethical plane. The noted scholars might be able to enlighten us further about the intellectual foundation of Sartrean ethics.

While it might be difficult to cater a good grasp of the Sartrean approach to moral philosophy by examining his posthumous releases, we could catch a glimpse into his mindset via these collections. We could learn about the theoretical foundation of these materials through the lenses of the noted prominent scholars. Their assessment of Sartre's works will show that Sartrean ethics exists, although it is underdeveloped.

From this point forward, my analysis will focus largely on the views echoed by the three scholars. I explore two major works: one is by Thomas Anderson and the other by Robert Stone and Elizabeth Bowman. Bear in mind that I refer to other publications during the discussions as well.

The work by Anderson assessed Sartre's early ethics. The author combined Sartre's first two ethics. He identified a few gaps in the reasoning. But Anderson fell short of denying that ethics.

The second work is by Stone and Bowman. These two authors looked at a series of notes, which Sartre prepared for several lectures, notably a lecture he was scheduled to deliver at Cornell University. Sartre never delivered that lecture.

The noted scholars agree that a Sartrean ethics exists. They are also convinced that such ethics is grounded in phenomenology. Sartre's written compositions in the ethical realm intertwine with his publications about phenomenological ontology. Many of his views about ethics are featured in the majestic work *Être et Le Néant* or *Being and Nothingness*.[1] These scholars suggest that the aptness of Sartrean ethics could be best examined through the lenses of existentialism. Let us explore their viewpoints further.

CHAPTER 9: A NEED TO GIVE SARTRE CREDIT

PLACING SARTREAN ETHICS

Jean-Paul Sartre deserves a place among moral philosophers. Although Sartre is known for his positions about existentialism, his fame also extends in ethics. But such a reputation does not come from negative criticisms about the nature of Sartrean ethics.

Critics argue that Sartre has no literary worth in ethics. But facets of his major literary achievements include relevant ethical parts. Even so, Sartre is not known for his exquisite treatises in ethics. Rather, he is mostly known as a failure in the ethical discipline.

Despite these views, I had a different lecture as I reviewed the writings of Thomas Anderson on the subject. I had a sense that Anderson agreed that there is a straight likeness between human morality and ethics in Sartre's writings. Anderson echoes that he found proof that Sartrean ethics exists, though that ethics is not perfect, he admitted. Let us explore Anderson's viewpoints in more detail.

Thomas Anderson points out that Sartre wrote extensively about ethical issues. He echoed that Sartre's moral thoughts evolved almost parallel to the ideas he proposed in existentialism. It might be hard to detach ethics in Sartre's written accomplishments, Anderson suggests.[2]

The foundation of Sartre's intellectual wealth relates his convictions about ethics. This view is rooted in Sartre's determination to examine or to appreciate the importance of the individual collaboration with *him-self* and the environment where he evolves. A human ethics plays a significant role in the foundation of existentialism.

The individual is always at the center of his actions. He must not only internalize such a link, but he must frame the interplay. From that understanding alone, one could not speak of an individual freedom without considering the role of individual ethics.

Ethical notions have played a central role in Sartre's career.[3] The characteristic of ethics could be found in various parts of the texts, which Sartre produced during his lifetime, including the materials, which he abstained from publishing himself about his moral concerns. His views transcended from an abstract idealistic ethics to a concrete, realistic, and possibly materialistic, morality.[4]

Ethics is relevant in Sartre's approach to notions of *value*, *sincerity*, and *being-in-and-for-itself*. All these achievements form a tool, which Sartre used to echo his ethical views.[5] But a Sartrean ethics is not as elusive as most pundits suggest. Ethics is embedded in the fundamental ideas, which Sartre intimated in his major works.

Describing Sartrean Ethics

Critics argue that Sartrean ethics is a farce. They say that avid Sartrean followers are determined to lift Sartre to an intellectual pedestal where he does not belong. But these analysts do not refute that Sartre produced many materials, which sketch out his ethical concerns.

Analysts are likely to question whether Sartre can be considered as a philosopher in ethics? The answer is not that complicated. By any measure, the answer is yes. This is undeniable, that is, even though pundits are quick to dismiss that likelihood.

The issue often debated is whether Sartre could deliver punchy thoughts in the ethical domain, as he did in other ways during his literary career. Many people say no. Most critics believe that Sartre was not a philosopher of ethical plumage. Nonetheless, critics offer incongruent explanations for their position, at least when it

Chapter 9: A Need To Give Sartre Credit

comes to the reason Sartre deserves no considerations in this literary discipline.

The notion that Sartre is not a philosopher in ethics is grounded on the presumption that Sartre did not have a developed ethics. The postulation is that, since Sartre had not produced materials, which adequately relayed his views about ethics, he could not embrace ethical issues the same way that he dominated other philosophical ideas. In my view, Sartre is cornered on all sides.

Even after Sartre wrote many essays, which address his concerns about important ethical issues, critics regard them as not enough. Such works could not place him as a prominent philosopher in morality. Sartre was not that philosopher, analysts resounded. The view espoused by observers is that it would be mistaken to think of Sartre as a pioneer in ethics.

I am not arguing that Sartre deserves to be considered as a great contributor in moral philosophy. But his intellect deserves more credit than it is currently afforded. In *Being and Nothingness*, Sartre laid out a powerful argument in favor of a human ontology. That argument reflects Sartre's ethical concerns. Even so, critics routinely overlook the Sartrean approach to moral philosophy.

In the noted book, Sartre described the ethical ramifications of human conducts. This work could help explain the Sartrean approach to an individual ethics. Even if Sartre did not elaborate on the ethical concerns, which reflect his views about human freedom, that reality would not provide any proof that such concerns are irrelevant.

Even though the nature of Sartrean ethical concerns (or his ideas in ethics) appear fragmented, they warrant further intellectual scrutiny. Despite the argument, which suggests this ethics is disjointed, the many writings, which Sartre published, both while alive and posthumously, are still relevant. The Sartrean mode of examining ethical issues deserves proper attentions, precisely when considering notions debating social mediation.[6]

It is true that little or no disputes exist about the degree to which Sartre had not produced a developed method, which would allow us to grasp his views. But that does not mean his approach is insignificant. That does not mean his literary achievements are inconsequential or should be considered that way.

Most of the voices, which opposed the idea of a Sartrean ethics, have also come from people who have projected little or no regards for Sartrean philosophy [as a whole]. If one were to consider arguments that are often proposed in the literature to counter Sartrean ethics, one would have to assume that Sartre had no philosophical worth at all. That would also implicate that one must refute any parts of the texts, which Sartre produced, not only about moral philosophy, but also in general.

This assertion might sound a little bit hyperbolic to some. But during my investigation of the literature about the topic, I found few pieces of scholarly works, which criticized Sartrean role in ethics, while lauding the excellence of Sartrean philosophy. I could not describe the scorn I discover about the fundamentals of Sartrean ethics during my research.

Another reality worth highlighting is that many of the views against Sartre are not in unison. Criticisms against Sartrean ethics are disjointed as well. Points of disputes are not always unanimous. While observers disagree with the idea that Sartre was incapable of producing valuable ideas about ethics, others have a different take.

Let us examine the materials, which Stone and Bowman compiled to explain this assertion further. They did take issue with the materials, which Sartre produced. But they did not reject the possibility that Sartre might play a relevant role in the ethical discipline. Unlike Thomas Anderson, Stone and Bowman provided a more descriptive assessment of the arguments, which I have echoed from beginning to end in this volume about the scope of Sartrean ethics.

THE ELUSIVE SARTREAN ETHICS

Robert Stone and Elizabeth Bowman suggest that a Sartrean approach to ethics is real. That ethics is grounded in societal issues. Their interjection in the debate highlights that a Sartrean philosophy has tentacles in ethics. Sartre's ideas about a human ontology are not only limited to the individual; there are other factors at play. Those factors emanate from the social environment itself.

The authors argue that there is a broader social context to consider when examining the extent of Sartrean ethics. Actions taken individually have larger social ramifications. Such actions become engrained in society.

This idea is in line with the viewpoint, which purports that existentialism and ethics enjoy a cooperative relationship. Of course, this dualism is often overlooked; else, it is artlessly ignored in the literature. Sartrean ethics is treated as a separate field of study, while existentialism is relegated to an introspective examination of the individual.

Supporters of the Sartrean approach emphasize the social ramifications of the ideas, which are presented in existentialism. Opponents see little or no connection between individual conducts and society or social institutions. The question worth asking is which of the two sides is right.

Depictions about the scope of Sartrean ethics are not cardinally an indication of how Sartre probably made out the role that ethics might play in solidifying individual conducts. But if we were to approach both individual ethics and general ethics from a dualism lens, it would be ineluctable to realize that there is no human ontology within Sartre's approach to human ethics. But Stone and Bowman have good reasons to hint that they support the idea that a Sartrean ethics exists. Their views did not emanate from hunches or other preferences. They assessed several documents, which Sartre prepared for a series of lectures he was scheduled to deliver at Cornell University.

These scholars note that Sartre evaluated morality in five ways in the newly uncovered materials. One could infer from their finds that both the individual and society are at the center of the Sartrean ethical model. Below is an excerpt of their reflections about the materials they reviewed.

They argue that Sartre had a clear interpretation of what he sought to suggest in his works. They further note that Sartrean ethics could be examined in the following manners.

Sartrean ethics could be judged in those terms

- By describing and fixing ethical conducts and structure within their specific characteristics
- By assessing whether ethics holds its own efficacy in the evolution of a political ensemble
- By assessing the foundations of ethical conducts and their internal laws
- By carrying out a progressive synthesis of the various foundational structures in an account of the contemporary practical agent
- By grasping the moral problem as it is revealed to this agent

Notes from: Stone and Bowman.[7]

Stone and Bowman note that phenomenology played an important role in proving the features of Sartrean ethics. Human ontology is the essentiality of Sartrean ethics, they imply. Thus, it is important to examine that ethics from an ontological lens. The role of phenomenology could be construed in the following manners.

Role of phenomenology in ethics
- Passive structure of everyday experience
- Ethics is (or can be) effective historically by itself

Notes from: Stone and Bowman.[8]

Third, these prominent scholars note the presence of social methods, which could be used in entirety as moral guidance. They argue that Sartrean ethics marks the role of social pressure onto individual conducts. A Sartrean perspective to ethics suggests that people could be influenced by duty. Those duties could take the form of imperatives, which may not be ethical.

Stone and Bowman further evaluate the nature of Sartre's written materials on the subject. They identify two types of imperatives. As it happens, these imperatives inform Sartrean ideas about ethics. They are as follows: categorical duties and hypothetical duties.

Types of imperatives	
Categorical duties	Hypothetical duties
• Universal and necessary	• Based on the object's own inclination

Notes from: Stone and Bowman.[9]

The previous discussion shows that Sartrean ethics is not elusive. This ethics is grounded in both the individual and society. But a specific fault worth pointing out is that it is not clear whether society influence individual conducts or whether an individual makes up his own conducts. Moreover, it is not clear the extent to which members of society must adjust because of individual conducts.

It is also uncertain the extent to which societies inform individual conducts. Perhaps individual conducts inform and guide society more than most would concede in the debate. Anyway, it would be inaccurate to deny any relationship between individual actions and society.

If we were to approach ethics as a separate field of study in Sartrean philosophy, a believable answer about the vivaciousness of ethics in individual conduct would be that societies settle such conducts. The individual must adjust to society's demands. The problem is that, from this end, there would be no individual freedom.

Sartre would not support such an approach to his philosophy about morality. Freedom is the trademark of the Sartrean philosophical brand. The human ontological project and human ethics are the same, or at least they function in tandem. This is the scheme of Sartrean philosophy; this is the theoretical foundation of Sartrean ethics.

Chapter Notes

[1] Stone and Bowman, "Sartre's Morality and History: A First Look at the Notes for the Unpublished 1965 Cornell Lectures."

[2] Anderson, Sartre's Two Ethics.

[3] Stone and Bowman, "Sartre's Morality and History: A First Look at the Notes for the Unpublished 1965 Cornell Lectures."

⁴ Anderson, *Sartre's Two Ethics*.

⁵ Stone and Bowman, "Sartre's Morality and History: A First Look at the Notes for the Unpublished 1965 Cornell Lectures."

⁶ Harold Bloom, *Jean-Paul Sartre* (Infobase Publishing, 2009).

⁷ Notes from: Stone and Bowman, "Sartre's Morality and History: A First Look at the Notes for the Unpublished 1965 Cornell Lectures," 57.

⁸ Notes from: Stone and Bowman, "Sartre's Morality and History: A First Look at the Notes for the Unpublished 1965 Cornell Lectures," 57.

⁹ Notes from: Stone and Bowman, "Sartre's Morality and History: A First Look at the Notes for the Unpublished 1965 Cornell Lectures," 57.

CHAPTER TEN

Sartre's Early Ethics

This chapter explores the extent of Sartre's early ethics. It reviews the significant points of disputes echoed in the literature about existentialism. The chapter examines the connection between intentional acts and the role of the being. This chapter assesses the role of the individual in the community. It reviews the intrinsic need of human beings to subject one another. It explores the heart of Sartrean ethics. The chapter examines Sartrean ethics over time. It shows a link between Sartre's early ethics and the views Sartre espoused in the unpublished materials. This section focuses [largely] on the views expressed by Thomas Anderson.

CHAPTER

10

A COMMONSENSE APPROACH

Sartre approached ethics from a commonsense perspective. Everything that he produced early in his career had a correlation with ethics. As Thomas Anderson notes, Sartre's early philosophical works led to the foundation of a realistic ethics.[1] This ethics change directions over the years.

From beginning to end, Sartre's early ethics experienced a metamorphic phase during Sartre's literary career. But this was mostly the case later in his life. While Sartre evolved as a philosopher, he became more entrenched in his own ideas or ideals. His views about the human ontology have also experienced an undeniable transformation.

The Sartrean stance about ethics mutated overtime. Anderson infers these changes could have come about because of Sartre's opinion about human reality and its relation to the world. Sartre sought to place the individual in the center of his philosophy. We could not undervalue the role of ethics in Sartre's approach to human conducts.

Anderson talks about Sartrean ethics in detail in his work. He argues that Sartre has always been attuned to the role that the individual played in construing his own views about freedom. Individual always framed the values he attaches to the need for freedom.

Moreover, Anderson explores the nature of Sartrean ethics. His views reinforce mine. Ethics and freedom are always intertwined. They are inseparable, one might say. Hence, Sartrean ethics could be best explored by examining the noted concepts in tandem. But we could only do so from the specific prism.

HISTORICAL FACTORS

Historical factors played a role in the evolution of Sartre's ideas. These factors, in turn, contributed to the change of his views overtime. Sartre's personal history has played a significant role in his positions. In the *Transcendence of the Ego*, for instance, Sartre began to layout his scheme for his stance about ethics.

Sartrean ethics is humanistic. [2] Videlicet, Sartre's understandings about ethics are grounded on his fundamental ideas about ontology (his interpretation of human conditions).[3] From this viewpoint, it could be said that ethics is grounded in the everyday issues, which the individual faces. No doubt, Sartre's approach to ethics delineates an individual reality.

A Sartrean outlook toward moral philosophy is grounded in Sartre's own life experience. His way of examining ethical issues, by much estimation, is political, social, and moral. Sartrean ethics is both practical and commonsensical.

Thomas Anderson notes that it is not necessary to have a philosophical foundation to have an "absolutely" positive ethics and politics. This argument suggests that the foundation of Sartrean ethics lies within his philosophy. From here, a Sartrean scrutiny of ethical issues centers on real problems, which is supposedly the underlying principle of his approach to human conducts. But there is more to the issues. Let us explore the different phases of Sartrean ethics.

EARLY ETHICS AND FREEDOM

Sartre sets up a morality that reflects human conditions. Arguing that notions referring to human reality had a major influence on Sartre's ethical outline is not far-fetched. Sartre's bearing to ethics is remarkably like his understandings about the role of the individual in setting up his place in the environment.

Thomas Anderson notes that we could understand Sartrean ethics by referencing three categories (*see* Figure 10.1).[4] They are as follows: idealistic, realistic, and Materialistic, and power and freedom.

Three Categories of Sartrean Ethics		
Idealistic	Realistic and Materialistic	Power and Freedom

Notes from: Thomas Anderson.[5]

CHAPTER 10: A COMMONSENSE APPROACH

Sartre's interest in phenomenology informed and guided his approach to ethical issues. Sartre was influenced by a realistic philosophy. What is more, Sartre concentrated on the philosophy that would allow him to describe objects just as he saw and touched them. It is unquestionable that examining the role of phenomenology in Sartrean ethics offers a significant insight into the foundation of Sartrean ethical model.

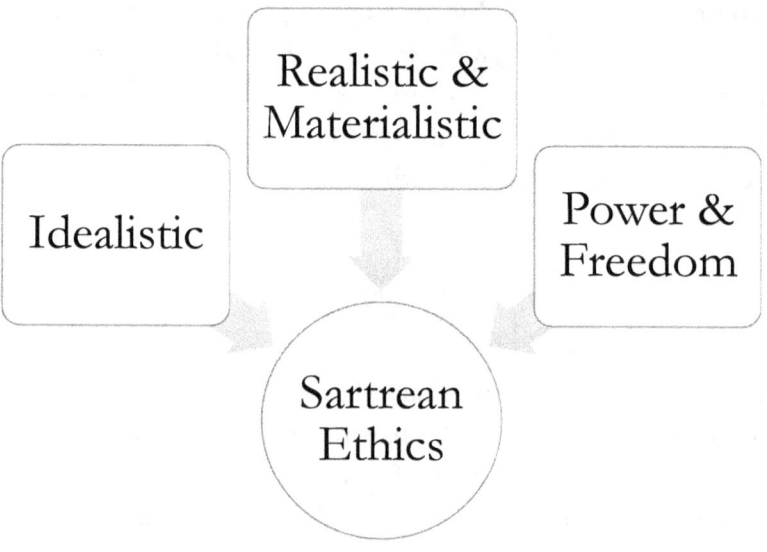

Figure 10. 1: Categories of Sartrean Ethics

Many of the commentators that, on any occasion appreciate what Jean-Paul Sartre had to offer as a brilliant philosopher, have explained a little skepticism about his ethics. Thomas Anderson suggests that Sartre's examination of ethics and the way he transported his views appeared hyperbolic and, at times, incomplete. Anderson notes that, often, Sartre exaggerated on his stance.

Anderson argues that the whole approach is abstract and incomplete. Sartre shows no real intimate interrelations between human beings and the world that they experience, as Sartre claims. There is much to expect between the theoretical and the practical sides of this ethics.

INTENTIONAL ACTS VERSUS BEING

Thomas Anderson seems unconvinced that Sartre proved a clear distinction between intentional acts and being. Anderson argues that intentional acts are not like a human being, even though Sartre used the terms interchangeably.[6] He further notes that objects of consciousness are not compulsorily the same as objects in the real world.

When Sartre speaks of *"Moi"* or *"The Self,"* he refers to intentional acts.[7] Anderson is also convinced that there is a clear distinction between the self and intentional acts. Anderson notes that the distinction Sartre sought to prove between psychic and physical characteristics is unclear.

This prominent Sartrean scholar believes that there is a reciprocal link between the world [within] and the world [outside]. Anderson is not sure whether Sartre successfully explained his ideas about the *"Moi"* or *"The Self."*[8] But Anderson came short of refuting the views, which Sartre explained in his works about ethics.

Sartre did not aptly grasp the concrete reality of men, Anderson notes. This lack of clarity poses a serious problem for settling the foundation of his ethics. There is the possibility that Sartre poorly understood the abstraction he expressed to use to explain his ethics toward human reality. Anderson argues that because Sartre used the terms *"consciousness," "man," "objects,"* and *"world"* interchangeably proves that he had no clue about the abstraction involved in his approach.[9]

AN ABSTRACT ETHICS

Thomas Anderson notes that, in many of his previous publications, Sartre stated that there is no way to resolve the world and consciousness.[10] The difference between the two is spontaneity. But spontaneity is not an object; rather, it is consciousness. Spontaneity is freedom.

Emotions play a role in consciousness. Anderson argues that the addition of emotions implicates the evolution of Sartre's conception of human reality and freedom. This is so from abstract to concrete.[11] I could refute facets of Anderson's viewpoints. But this is not my primary objective here.

In refuting parts of Anderson's argument, we might find it necessary to appeal to the argument Sartre elaborated in *Being and Nothingness*. It would become obvious that Sartre sought to detach himself from the abstract toward a more concrete understanding of the man.[12] He tried to balance between human reality and freedom.

Sartre divides reality into two realms: *"consciousness"* and *"non-consciousness things."* Sartre admits that consciousness is nothing but intentional acts. They are about the world we experience.

Sartre restates that spontaneity of consciousness is self-determining; it is the cause of itself. It can be self-activated. Non-conscious things are passive and inert. The exhibition of being [in itself] is what we experience; it is both being and non-being.[13]

Examining the Role of Consciousness

Thomas Anderson further notes that because consciousness is always present to *itself*, it cannot coincide with *itself*. The apperception of a passive or an empty distance between the self and consciousness allows the self to be for itself or self-conscious. This is the foundation of a man's freedom, Anderson argues.[14]

Considering bad faith—that is, the relationship individuals have to themselves, with themselves, and for themselves—Anderson notes that the freedom, which Sartre echoes in his major literary achievements is the freedom that allows the individual the capacity to make choices, or the freedom to select among goals. In substance, this is the freedom of consciousness.[15]

When it comes to the speculations echoed about *"human emotions,"* Anderson disagrees that all emotions and passions are free. He notes that the mere fact that those acts or feelings are intentional does not mean that they are free per se. Anderson further notes that certain emotions or desires are indeed free (for example, sexual desire).[16] But most desires are conditional responses, which had been provoked by made out realities or imagined objects, Anderson argues. A person does not decide the types of emotions he feels at any given time. One often experiences fear whether one chooses to feel that way.

Anderson notes that Sartre's view about the inkling of freedom came from his understanding of the role of facticity in settling human conduct. He further notes that the role of other situations in which one has little or no control over his destiny. From this viewpoint, there is no complete freedom.

Anderson wonders whether a Sartrean approach to freedom is misleading. He notes that when it comes to human relation and ethics, total freedom could create a situation where conflicts would be unavoidable. Thus, according to Thomas Anderson, freedom is not always attainable. If it were to be, then it would implicate the individual at the most conscious state of self.

The author notes that because humans have an intrinsic desire to dominate and subjugate one another, this poses serious implications for Sartrean ethics. He suggests that the whole point of ethics contradicts the idea of freedom.[17] Note that Anderson did not refute Sartrean ethics in his scrutiny of Sartre's literary imprints. A good portion of the observations that Thomas Anderson made about the Sartrean approach to ethics are, *de facto*, valid, I would argue.

ASSESSING THE ESSENCE OF SARTREAN ETHICS

Various parts of the *"for-itself"* can be used to explain the object of an existential psychoanalysis.[18] Thomas Anderson ponders on the essence of an ethics if consciousness needs an objectification of the other. Because the extemporization of consciousness or subjectivity plays a significant role in human relations, one is inevitably a subject or an object, depending on the perspective of the person being objectified or else.

To avoid alienation or degradation, people often resort to ruse. The individual cannot control the way that others judge him or the way he judges others. This view does not refute Jean-Paul Sartre in ethics per se. Manifestly, it is not clear whether it indispensably denies the role of Sartrean ethics. But it reinforces many of the ideas relayed in previous sections about the extent of that ethics.

We could agree that Sartrean ethics is not in a perfect state. There are issues that raise questions. My arguments were not designed to refute criticisms. Instead, I argue in favor of conviviality in the debate. But it must be noted that Thomas

Anderson is proof of that conviviality and academic civility. I would echo that view vigorously.

Thomas Anderson assessed the role of values and norms in Sartrean ethics. He recognized that ethics would affect individual freedom. Anderson examined the Sartrean model. Despite his disagreements, Anderson fell short of trashing the Sartrean approach to ethics. He displayed an uncanny intellectual fair play, which, in my view, is lacking in the current discourse about Sartrean ethics.

In the Sartrean world, both the need to strengthen certain values and the need to gain freedom go together. The moral agent, which is the individual himself, is the cornerstone of the types of values that he espouses. The being is governed by ethical concerns.

Because people want to exist by right and not by chance, being or playing God becomes the supreme goal to achieve value. This intrinsic attitude could eventually affect human ethics. Thomas Anderson further asks what the point of ethics is [or could be] is if all men aspire to the same goal. I am not sure how to respond. But I am certain that Sartre would offer a rebuttal to Anderson's puzzling remarks and queries, had he been alive.

Anderson notes that ethics is supposed to help human beings in their search to live a good life. This is so, despite their eventual failure to reach the freedom that they are seeking in life. Anderson recognizes the role of ethics in human freedom. Sadly, this is a fact that most analysts refute.

In sum, Thomas Anderson argues that early Sartrean ethics did not do a good job in making a case for freedom, notably the types of freedom Sartre proposed in *Being and Nothingness*. He further notes that Sartre did not suggest a clear signal that he mastered the ethical implications of his approach to freedom.[19] Still, Anderson never denies the relevance of that ethics per se.

Anderson recognizes that Sartrean ethics has some intellectual relevance. These are the arguments, which I have been trying to underline in the present text. Anderson's arguments provide a well-needed credence to my points of strife in the present context.

Chapter Notes

[1] Anderson, Sartre's Two Ethics.

[2] Ibid.

[3] Ibid.

[4] Ibid., 105–106.

[5] Ibid., 105–106.

[6] Anderson, Sartre's Two Ethics.

[7] Ibid.

[8] Ibid.

[9] Ibid.

[10] Ibid.

[11] Ibid.

[12] Sartre, Being and Nothingness.

[13] Anderson, Sartre's Two Ethics.

[14] Ibid.

[15] Ibid.

[16] Ibid.

[17] Ibid.

[18] Sartre, Existentialism and Human Emotion.

[19] Anderson, Sartre's Two Ethics.

CHAPTER ELEVEN

Ethics and Society

This chapter focuses on the views expressed by Robert Stone and Elizabeth Bowman. It evaluates the intellectual authority of Sartre's early positions about ethics. It examines the way individual freedom may affect society. The chapter elaborates on how society and individuals interact on the ethical plane. The examination centers on how the individual affects society. It explores how society affects the individual in similar manner. It discusses how existentialism is dominated by ethical notions. The chapter closes by stressing on the irrefutable relationship between ethics and human ontology.

CHAPTER

11

THE EFFECTS OF SOCIETY

In the first ethics (as outlined in *The Notebooks for an Ethics*), Sartre has taken a different approach to human freedom. Thomas Anderson argues that Sartre considered the social elements, which could hamper individual freedom. Sartre also argues that human beings are not pure consciousness.

Sartre would say that the individual is immersed, invested in facticity. Thus, the individual is concretely placed in the world. From a non-objective lens, the body plays a role in freedom. My body makes my freedom; that freedom is implicitly concrete and qualified.[1]

Sartre further argues that people transcend and regret the facticity in their situation. Factors such as economies, status, works, personal qualities, or other factors proscribe the limits of choices, which could effectively undermine freedom. Sartre notes that people can be both *"determined"* and *"free."*[2]

Sartre holds that all human beings are free by nature. The human freedom is the science of meaning and value.[3] But individual value is not first his (own) freedom, but that of others. It is conceivable that human beings do not enjoy freedom after all. As an illustration, other forces could be acting on that freedom. There is a constant struggle to be free. The individual must strive for freedom.

Freedom and Society

Notions of freedom are informed by society. Robert Stone and Elizabeth Bowman note that in social settings, directions are used as a tool to impose rigidity on present actions. But within the Sartrean ethics, these directions are called imperatives. Workers, for instance, are compelled to work or to live within these categorical imperatives. If a person wants to live a respectable life and to earn a living, he must do this or that, among other realities.[4]

In a social setting, workers are trapped into this circle of dependence. Their dependence to social norms and social structure becomes their present, past, and future. The system imposes a certain destiny on them. They must accept it. Even though workers may hate their situation, they have little or no choice, but to uphold them.

Stone and Bowman argue that it is an ethical determination. Other imperatives also place duties onto people. For instance, you must vote. As a result, the individual has little or no choice but to engage in the polity of the land.

Stone and Bowman identify the role of the media in Sartrean ethics. The press plays an important role in gathering, systemizing, and reflecting popular ethics or ideals.[5] The press conventionally puts itself at the service of political ends. But once those norms have been accepted, they can be difficult to destroy.[6]

Society Affects Ethics

We could understand Sartrean ethics by evoking social norms. Certain norms become pre-reflexive social structures. Therefore, they may take urgent forms. Ethics is a historical reality, which is grounded in history. For the same reason, such ethics may become the result of historical determinations.

Social and historic factors could coincide with social or political actions. In such a way, individual actions could be guided by a certain moral virtue. The authors cite an example in West Virginia (during the 1960s), where many people voted for a moral virtue, which, at the time, various social problems required a different path. Political choices were tied with ethical motives.

A Sartrean approach to ethics suggests that the term itself is not without limits. Despite social constraints, Sartre would argue that there is always an element of freedom at play. In the previous example, the implication of freedom was overtly obvious.

Sartrean ethics suggests that even though there were certain political or social determinations at play in West Virginia, the people still expressed their freedom in the political act of voting. Ethics played an important role in the decision to vote.

ETHICAL NORMATIVE

Stone and Bowman note that Sartre stressed on the compulsion of ethics in the daily life of the individual. Norms are lived in the dialectical sense.[7] But norms could aim at regulating human relationships. In the same vein, ethical models may settle human relations.

Institutions, customs, values, an exemplary conduct, and ideals play a significant role in how people make out their role in society. It is prevailingly understood that institutions, namely, the state, languages, and property, often decide people's conducts through imperatives. The law sets the duties and rights in society. to give an instance, people must uphold them.

Mores are acts that are preeminently required by customs.[8] Those mores create sanctions or social disapproval, which in turn create individual duty to conform. Values are important because of the types of relationship they enjoy among people.

The value of sincerity set the boundary for lying. You must not lie. But that does not mean that the individual would never lie.

Values can regulate individual conducts as well. To sketch that idea, Sartre echoes that exemplary conducts may encourage people to engage in the right conducts.[9] Ethics guides people, through norms, for sure, in a systematic movement toward an end.[10]

MUTUAL RECOGNITION

A Sartrean view of ethics suggests that it is a mutual recognition of subjectivity. As illustrated in the previous chapter, Thomas Anderson highlights several issues with early Sartrean ethics. He notes that Sartre failed to set up that consciousness is not one to itself. But ethics, in and of itself, contradict any notions of freedom.

Anderson suggests that, in his early publications, Sartre did not patently explain his ethical views in a way that considered social factors. Certain moral principles are intrinsically against ideals of changes. Stone and Bowman proved that Sartre developed a different approach to ethics toward the end of his career. These authors identified what Sartre called *"The Paradox of Ethics."* Ends of actions are inseparable from the structures and the process of making oneself a subject of interiority. One makes oneself subject to interiority by aiming at some precise end.

Let us consider a child tells the truth to his parent. Sartrean ethics suggests that he is seeking to maximize the value of sincerity. That action, however, is restricted by certain moral values. Sartre notes that to understand why people act in a certain way, we must grasp what people lack and what they are seeking in the world.

MORALITY AND LACK

Fundamentally, a *"lack"* may explain the need, which people often have so they could get what they lack. The being is inclined to seek what he needs or what he may perceive as a need. It seems fitting to intimate that a moral entity does not lose all notions of freedom.[11]

In *Being and Nothingness*, Sartre argues that human beings are essentially free, except when in bad faith. Even so, in many levels of ourselves, we are ignorant of ourselves.[12] Bad faith could be unavoidable. In this way, the individual is sometimes obligated to appeal to bad faith to be free or to survive in the world.

In his early writings, Sartre assessed the question of identity. He argued that the individual is in a constant search for identity.

Because civil society demands repression, the individual cannot be allowed to function independently. Yet, being in society also demands a form of freedom. Individual freedom, on the other hand, is constantly hampered by society. It seems like there is a constant struggle between individual needs and collective needs or desire.

The individual is always aware of the self. He cannot stop his subjectivity. But this is a violation of the principle of identity, Sartre hinted. Anytime the individual thinks of the self as a fixed reality, he is in bad faith.

Thomas Anderson points out that in his early essays, Sartre struggled to prove a clear divide between individual freedom and collective freedom. He failed to consider the influence of the collectivity on individual freedom. Later in his career, Sartre abandoned the characteristic of individual freedom altogether.

Although Sartre never embraced communism, he seemed confused about what he originally stood for, as Anderson points out. Anderson further notes that understandings about an individual freedom had been seeping away from Sartre's consciousness. In his relatively recent texts about ethics, Sartre seemed concerned with collective freedom.

The notion of freedom is the foundation of Sartrean ethics. The same could be said about the role ethics play in Sartre's approach to human ontology. With that understanding settled, let me wrap up the arguments echoed throughout this book. Let me remind you of my central thesis.

Chapter Notes

[1] Anderson, *Sartre's Two Ethics*.

[2] Ibid.

3 Ibid.

4 Stone and Bowman, "Sartre's Morality and History: A First Look at the Notes for the Unpublished 1965 Cornell Lectures."

5 Ibid.

6 Ibid.

7 Ibid.

8 Ibid.

9 Ibid.

10 Ibid.

11 Ibid.

12 Anderson, Sartre's Two Ethics.

Chapter 11: The Effects Of Society

Chapter Twelve

A New Paradigm

Existentialism is plagued with ethical ramifications. They include the role of norms, mutual recognition, and morality or the lack of that. Therefore, ethics and human ontology go together. There is a need to reevaluate criticisms against Jean-Paul Sartre in the ethical discipline. I call for a positive scrutiny of the documents, which Sartre produced about ethics. I reflect on the degree to which I carried out my goals in defending Jean-Paul Sartre.

CHAPTER

12

A Call for a Better Approach

There is no doubt that Jean-Paul Sartre enjoyed an influence on Western philosophy. His literary contributions in contemporary literature have helped outshine traditional views about the importance of human ontology. Sartre's ideas discussing the extent of human existence have revolutionized popular impressions about the weight of ethics.

When I speak of Sartrean ethics, I am referring to the concept known as phenomenology. It intertwines with Sartre's approach to human ontology. Sartre is a pioneer in phenomenology. The fundamental question is whether Sartre is a philosopher in ethics.

Chapter 12: A Call For A Better Approach

The arguments I highlighted here center on the idea that Sartre deserves such a title. Granted, this view is in the minority. Sartrean ethics is not fully developed.

Critics do not automatically reject the prolegomenon that Sartre had a major influence on popular culture. But few observers share the belief that Sartre left a permanent mark in the ethical realm. This understanding is contradictory, to say the least, to the reality at hand. In this instance, only the opposite is true.

The presupposition is that Sartre did not have a fully developed set of moral precepts in his writings, which would make him eligible for considerations as a philosopher in ethics. Critics are convinced that it would be an error to consider Sartre as a worthy contributor in ethics. I disagree. This is a misguided view of Sartre's valor in the ethical discipline.

Mistaken Viewpoints

The views often explained in the literature are grounded on the theory that, Sartre did not produce enough relevant ideas about ethics.[5] Sartre produced many relevant materials that could be useful to the field. Thus, Sartre deserves credit for his contribution to moral philosophy.

I am not arguing that these materials are enough to turn him into an expert in ethics. I am merely suggesting that Sartre deserves credit for his publications about ethics. The materials, which Sartre produced to illustrate his concerns about ethics, have an intellectual merit. To put it another way, we should not undermine these publications or put them aside because of impulsive reasons alone.

---

[5] I am referring to the publication argument.

Opponents contend that it would be superfluous to regard Jean-Paul Sartre as someone who deserves any considerations as a contributor in ethical writings. But these kinds of criticisms do not always come from occasional readers or misinformed dissenters. Such views come from men and women of letters. For good reasons, I am perturbed about the possible motives, which may lead to such misjudgments toward Jean-Paul Sartre.

Scholars of all creeds [or expertise] in philosophical writings agree that Sartre was not successful in laying down the foundation of his ideas in moral philosophy. But the extent to which they depicted the property of Sartrean ethics was not the primary goal of this book. The arguments centered on the contemplation that Sartre could be considered a moral philosopher, despite the scope of both his published and unpublished materials.

A Positive Scrutiny of Sartrean Ethics

Critics have a different approach about Sartrean ethics. They regard that ethics differently. These people include scholars and non-scholars alike. They say that Sartre delivered a stunning examination of the individual via the existentialist model. They echo that Sartrean ethics could be best examined through the lens of existentialism. These two concepts are interlaced. I agree.

Other analysts hold the view that Sartre did not excel in ethics with the same zeal, which he laid down the ground for his theory about human ontology. Most observers, including Sartrean scholars and non-scholars, support the view that a Sartre's version of ethics is an elusive concept. I sought to refute that claim.

In the present compilation, I sought to show the roots of Sartrean ethics; that ethics is plain; it can be found in Sartre's major literary works. While that ethics is not developed, it deserves recognition. Denying the Sartrean approach to ethics to such an extent could be considered an ethical matter in and of itself.

The debate about the scope of Sartrean ethics would best serve the literature if it were centered on whether Sartre matches other great philosophers, not, by its own nature, whether Sartre had any standing as a moral philosopher. It is immaterial whether Sartre had a convincingly developed ethics. What is important is the acknowledgment that Sartre contributed to the field.

SARTREAN ETHICS AND HUMAN EXISTENCE

Another reality to note in the debate is that it is important to recognize that Sartre examined the human existence from various angles. On the one hand, he explored the being from an ontological perspective. On the other hand, he catalogued the being from an ethical lens.

Despite views to the contrary, Sartre is a philosopher in morality. He is a moralist in all his glory. Sartre has in irrefutable approach to ethics. Thus, Sartre played a significant role in the ethical discipline. Of course, the previous viewpoints are in the minority. Certainly, viewpoints to the contrary are always debatable.

The intransigence toward Sartre and his views about morality is obvious. Few analysts see a link between Sartrean philosophy and Sartrean ethics. The point of disputation often sketched is that Sartre's approach to existentialism differs from his written viewpoints about ethics. Ethics played little or no role in the ontological examination of individual conducts, critics argued. But how is this possible?[1]

The study of the individual would invariably invite an evaluation of moral values. Existentialism seems intertwined with ethical notions. Any scrutiny of the individual would inextricably involve a scrutiny of his ethics. There is no denying it; the presence of ethical concerns is undeniable in ontology. The Sartrean approach to ontology is useless without advising his examination of morality.

The point of strife echoed here shown inside and out throughout this text is that the underpinnings of existentialism seem grounded in Sartre's own views about moral philosophy. Portions of Sartrean philosophy are filled with ethical notions. But it was necessary to point out that, unfortunately, this is not the way most critics consider the issues. For them, there is no ethics to be had in Sartrean ethics. Notwithstanding what we know now about Sartrean ethics, this understanding is absurd in and of itself.

Sartre produced several materials about ethics; they are worthy of merit. Yes, authorities who oppose this idea are swift to rebuke the theorem that Sartrean ethics could merge with existentialism. The present work challenged that view fervently.

Carrying Out My Goals

Jean-Paul Sartre invariably recorded his ethical views. He did so in many ways. Sartre regularly outlined the foundation for his ethical thoughts, although his ideas were uncompleted. But to discover whether Sartre deserves the title of a relevant thinker in ethics, one does not have to look further than his writings about existentialism. This might be the simplest way to appreciate relevant sides of Sartrean ethics.

In *Existentialism and Human Emotions*, Sartre suggested parts of his ethics clearly. He echoed that there is an irrefutable link between human ontology and human ethics. Sartre warns that the "Ontology itself cannot formulate ethical precepts." [2] This approach, as a stand-alone philosophical precept, is clearly a technique, which affords an unfiltered examination of the extent of human ethics.

The human reality could be best understood through the lenses of ontology. Human ethics can be assessed by exploring the way the individual reacts to his reality in each situation.[3] That is why human ontology can help us decipher how the individual sets up values or the lack of that.

Sartre contends that his theory about existentialism has inescapable ethical implications. In effect, "Existential psychoanalysis is a moral description," Sartre further notes.[4] Human beings normally nourish certain preconceived suppositions about their role in their environment.[5]

With all these means, existentialism "releases to us the ethical meaning of various human projects."[6] Ontology reveals to us, "the ideal of meaning of all human attitudes."[7] Human beings construe their own universe and create their own reality within it. To that extent, ethics is the essence of men.

We could appreciate human reality distinctively by examining how the man makes out himself in the world. Sartre argues that man wants to be God. But to carry out that goal, "*egoism*" or "*self-interest*" becomes a feature of the man, not a glitch.

The individual must create the conditions for his existence. Therefore, "Man loses himself the self-cause may exist."[8] That self-cause is emotionally ethical.

Chapter Notes

[1] In the Notebooks for an Ethics (1992), Sartre attempted to develop an ethics that is on par with ideas evoked in the profound individualism of his existential philosophy.

[2] Sartre, Existentialism and Human Emotion, 91.

[3] Sartre, Existentialism and Human Emotion.

[4] Ibid., 91.

[5] Ibid., 91.

[6] Ibid.

[7] Sartre, Existentialism and Human Emotion.

[8] Ibid., 92.

Chapter 12: A Call For A Better Approach

CONCLUSION

Closing Thoughts

This section wraps up our discussion. It reasserts the ideas voiced throughout the text. The section restates the key positions I advanced in favor of Jean-Paul Sartre as a moral philosopher. It examines the intellectual relevance of Sartre's major writings about ethics. It restates the central thesis echoed in the book.

Final Words

Does Jean-Paul Sartre have any relevance in moral philosophy? The answer is YES. I provided enough evidence to support that view. But I refuted any viewpoint to the contrary. I rejected views that refute Sartrean ethics without tangible proofs.

Why defending Sartrean ethics, you might ask. But why not, I would ask you in return. Anyway, I sought to defend Jean-Paul Sartre for various reasons, some of which I did not find necessary to mention here. By force of circumstances, that defense was not exhaustive. I wanted to share my viewpoints as coherently as possible in the debate.

While compiling this work, I found myself reflecting on various abstract ideas. When I stumbled on the writings of Jean-Paul Sartre, I thought I had uncovered a novel approach to understand others and myself more efficiently. I must admit that Sartrean philosophy had a marked impact on me.

I had a primitive appreciation of Sartrean philosophy. My approach was archaic. My idea of existentialism was relegated to ill-conceived notions about human existence. I thought existentialism was the answer to the age-old question, "Why are we here?"

Final Words

As I learned about the ideas that Sartre echoed in his essays, I became more inquisitive about the notion of freedom. But the existentialist model did not answer all my questions. There were many puzzling issues about human ontology, which I could not find out on my own. Examining the materials, which Sartre produced, provided interesting insights, which also played an important role in my intellectual growth.

Initially, I approached Sartrean ethics as a separate entity. I treated the role of ethics as an independent facet of Sartrean philosophy. But I could not see a clear divide between the two ideas. Now, I have a different understanding of the philosophy, which Jean-Paul Sartre pioneered during his lengthy literary career.

Wrapping-Up the Debate

Existentialism could help decipher the way that individuals frame their place in the world. It could help us understand how the individuals could carve out their reality as they see fit. In my view, notions debating existentialism and ethics are similar. If not, they overlap. But it is always best to examine important ethical implications by exploring the existentialist model. The opposite is also true, I would contend.

An undeniable link exists between the Sartrean approach to existentialism and the Sartrean view about certain ethical notions. It is definite that, to the surprise of single-minded pundits, Sartre addressed these links eloquently in his literary productions. Any refutation against that argument could derive from a hasty, if not a subjective, assessment of the works, which Sartre produced about ethics.

As a stand-alone field of study, ethics would be hard to decipher. It would be so from a Sartrean prism. Without a good understanding of the ideas Sartre communicated about human ontology, it might be difficult to grapple important ethical notions.

Sartrean philosophy and ethics must be examined in tandem. This is a position I am willing to abandon if I became convinced of Sartre's irrelevance in the ethical discipline. But as of now, this possibility seems unlikely.

The views echoed in this volume are in the minority. I am not the only one who could grasp Sartrean ethics. I do not proclaim any epistemological propriety over Sartre's writings about ethics, inclusively when it comes to his views about philosophy. For all that, this publication reflects my own interpretation of the issues.

My point is that the present work reflects my understanding of the growing debate about the scope of Sartrean ethics. It could also be a testimony of my ignorance about the subject. But I will let you (the reader) be the judge of that.

THE FOUNDATION OF THIS BOOK

Many years ago, I enrolled in a semester-long course about philosophy.[1] I learned a lot from the course. Because of that experience, I became interested in learning more about several philosophical ideas, including human ontology. Along the way, I amassed other insights that could explicate this seemingly brave try to defend a man who found himself cornered from all angles.

I recently attended another course about philosophy. That course was about Jean-Paul Sartre.[2] The professor explored several sides of Sartrean ethics. I was incredibly pleased to have taken these courses.

I sought to defend the Sartrean legacy. But I hoped to do so by pointing out ill-conceived criticisms. My goal was to interject intellectual civility in the current debate. Because of my academic experience, I not only had the opportunity to reacquaint myself with several of Sartre's major philosophical principles, but I was also exposed to his approach to ethics.

I wanted to share that experience with you. Whether I succeeded in this strive is up to you. I sincerely hope that I was able to convey my arguments in the text expertly and as convincingly as possible. I hope this book was informative and intellectually captivating.

Chapter Notes

[1] This class was taught by Dr. Glen A. Mazis. He is a professor of philosophy at the Pennsylvania State University.

[2] This class was taught by Dr. Thomas W. Busch. He is a professor of philosophy at Villanova University.

APPENDICES

Selected Works about Jean-Paul Sartre

This section introduces the appendices, which include several recent publications about Jean-Paul Sartre. This section features several selected books about Sartre. It features selected articles, academic journals, newspapers, and magazines dedicated to Sartre and Simone de Beauvoir. The book culminates with a miscellaneous part.

APPENDICES

Jean-Paul Sartre has constantly been the subject of intense scrutiny. Since he died (in 1980), many scholars have written about his legacy and his philosophy. As noted in the introductory part, many of the publication, which had been logged about Sartre, are critical in explaining the Sartrean philosophy.

Other publications have been less critical and have praised Sartre for his many contributions to human literature. In 2014, for instance, Thomas Flynn published a marvelous piece of literature about Sartre. The book is titled *Sartre: A Philosophical Biography*.

There have been several types of publications about Sartre. Observers pointed out the flaws in his philosophical stance. Other works have been more neutral. They highlight Sartre literary prowess, notably in several literary discipline.

The next portion of the manuscript features several publications about Jean-Paul Sartre. But I only focus on two years (2005 and 2006). During those years, there had been a plethora of literary items, which are dedicated to Sartre.

Let me say that focusing on just two years is to underline that Sartre defied the notion that a genie only has one century to be relevant.[6] Seemingly, Sartre defied the "One-century-per-genie" model. He remains the subject of literary scrutiny.

The next few pages highlight literary items that others published about Sartre. They include books, academic journals, magazines, and newspapers. Below is a list of a few selected books about Sartre. Please note this list is not exhaustive.

---

[6] "Le Génie N'a Qu'un Siècle, Après Quoi, Il Faut Qu'il Dégénère."

APPENDIX A: SELECTED BOOKS

SELECTED BOOKS ABOUT SARTRE (2005-2006)

Title	Author(s)	Publisher	Date
Sartre's Nausea: Text, Context, Intertext	Alistair Rolls; Elizabeth Rechniewski	Rodopi	2005
Jean-Paul Sartre and the Jewish Question: Anti-Antisemitism and the Politics of the French Intellectual	Jonathan Judaken	University of Nebraska Press	2006
Forms in the Abyss: A Philosophical Bridge between Sartre and Derrida	Steve Martinot	Temple University Press	2006
Ontology and Ethics in Sartre's Early Philosophy	Yiwei Zheng	Lexington Books	2005

Selected Works About Jean-Paul Sartre

APPENDIX B: SELECTED MAGAZINES

SELECTED MAGAZINES ABOUT SARTRE (2005-2006)

Title	Author(s)	Publisher	Volume	Date
Food: Camus Knew How to Clean Chickpeas- One More Reason to Prefer Him to Sartre	Roberts, Michele	New Statesman (1996)	Vol. 134, No. 4732	March 21, 2005
An Atheist on the 'Compost of Catholicity': Remembering Jean-Paul Sartre on His Centennial	King, Thomas M.	National Catholic Reporter	Vol. 41, No. 32	June 17, 2005
A Groovy Pair	Roberts, Michele	New Statesman (1996)	Vol. 135, No. 4776	January 23, 2006

Selected Works About Jean-Paul Sartre

APPENDIX C: SELECTED ACADEMIC JOURNALS

ACADEMIC JOURNALS ABOUT SARTRE (2005-2006)

Title	Author(s)	Publisher	Volume	Date
Sartre's Ethics of the Oppressed	Mann, Anika	Philosophy Today	Vol. 49	2005
Sartre as Philosopher of the Imagination	Flynn, Thomas	Philosophy Today	Vol. 50	2005
Sartre's Response to Merleau-Ponty's Charge of Subjectivism	Bernasconi, Robert	Philosophy Today	Vol. 50	2006
Sartre and the Virtual: A Deleuzian Interpretation of the Transcendence of the Ego	Somers-Hall, Henry	Philosophy Today	Vol. 50	2006
Quest for Identity in Richard Wright's the Outsider: An Existentialist Approach	Abdurrahman, Umar	The Western Journal of Black Studies	Vol. 30, No. 1	Spring 2006
Sartre, Critical Theory, and the Paradox of Freedom	Sherman, David	Philosophy Today	Vol. 50, No. 2,	Summer 2006
Sartre and the Communicative Paradigm in Critical Theory	Berendzen, J. C.	Philosophy Today	Vol. 50, No. 2	Summer 2006

Tête-à-tête : Simone de Beauvoir and Jean-Paul Sartre	Glazer, Sarah	Women's Studies Quarterly	Vol. 34, No. 3/4	Fall 2006

APPENDIX D: SELECTED NEWSPAPERS

SELECTED NEWSPAPERS ABOUT SARTRE (2005-2006)

Title	Author(s)	Publisher	Location	Date
Airbrushing History	N/A	The Washington Times	Washington, DC	March 12, 2005
All Very Stylish but Sartre's Vision Is Still Hell on Earth	Mountford, Fiona	The Evening Standard	London, England	September 6, 2005
Of a Legendary, Eccentric 20th-Century Love Affair	Rubin, Martin	The Washington Times	Washington, DC	October 9, 2005

BIBLIOGRAPHY

Anderson, Thomas C. "Beyond Sartre's Ethics of Authenticity." *Journal of the British Society for Phenomenology* 33, no. 2 (January 1, 2002): 138–54. doi:10.1080/00071773.2002.11007376.

———. *Sartre's Two Ethics: From Authenticity to Integral Humanity*. Chicago, Ill: Open Court Publishing Company, 1993.

Aronson, Ronald, and Adrian Van Den Hoven, eds. *Sartre Alive*. Detroit: Wayne State University Press, 1991.

Becker, Lawrence C., and Charlotte B. Becker. *Encyclopedia of Ethics*. Routledge, 2013.

Bernstein, Richard J. *Praxis and Action: Contemporary Philosophies of Human Activity*. University of Pennsylvania Press, 2011.

Bloom, Harold. *Jean-Paul Sartre*. Infobase Publishing, 2009.

Bourg, Julian. *From Revolution to Ethics: May 1968 and Contemporary French Thought*. McGill-Queen's Press - MQUP, 2007.

Detmer, David. *Freedom as a Value: A Critique of the Ethical Theory of Jean-Paul Sartre*. La Salle, Ill: Open Court Publishing Company, 1988.

Flynn, Thomas. "Jean-Paul Sartre." In *The Stanford Encyclopedia of*

Philosophy, edited by Edward N. Zalta, Fall 2013., 2013. http://plato.stanford.edu/archives/fall2013/entries/sartre/.

Guyau, Jean-Marie. *A Sketch of Morality Independent of Obligation Or Sanction*. Watts, 1898.

Heidegger, Martin. *Discourse on Thinking: A Translation of Gelassenheit*. Translated by John M. Anderson and E. Hans Freund. New York: Harper & Row, 1966.

Heter, T. Storm. "Authenticity and Others: Sartre's Ethics of Recognition." *Sartre Studies International: An Interdisciplinary Journal of Existentialism and Contemporary Culture* 12, no. 2 (2006): 17.

Ji, Ruman. "Freedom: The Unifying Thread of Sartre's Ethics." DePaul University, 1998.

"Le Génie N'a Qu'un Siècle, Après Quoi, Il Faut Qu'il Dégénère." Accessed October 20, 2015. http://www.linternaute.com/citation/13020/le-genie-n-a-qu-un-siecle--apres-quoi--il-faut-qu-il---voltaire/.

Sartre, Jean-Paul. *Anti-Semite and Jew: An Exploration of the Etiology of Hate*. Translated by George J. Becker. New York: Schocken, 1995.

———. *Being and Nothingness*. Translated by Hazel E. Barnes. Reprint edition. New York: Washington Square Press, 1993.

———. *Cahiers pour une morale*. Paris: Gallimard, 1983.

———. *Existentialism and Human Emotion*. Reissue edition. New York: Citadel, 1987.

———. *Notebooks for an Ethics*, 1992.

Sartre, Jean-Paul, and Steven Ungar. *"What Is Literature?" And Other Essays*. Third Printing edition. Cambridge, Mass: Harvard University Press, 1988.

Schilpp, Paul Arthur. *The Philosophy of Jean-Paul Sartre*. Open Court, 1981.

Stone, Robert V., and Elizabeth Bowman A. "Sartre's Morality and History: A First Look at the Notes for the Unpublished 1965 Cornell Lectures." In *Sartre Alive*, 53–82. Detroit: Wayne State University Press, 1991.

Recommended Readings

Anderson, Thomas C. "Sartre's Early Ethics and the Ontology of Being Ad Nothingness." In *Sartre Alive*, 183–201. Detroit: Wayne State University Press, 1991.

An Investigation of Jean-Paul Sartre's Posthumously Published Notebooks for an Ethics. Lewiston, N.Y: Edwin Mellen Pr, 2000.

Appignanesi, Lisa. "Did Simone de Beauvoir's Open 'Marriage' Make Her Happy?" *The Guardian*, June 10, 2005, sec. World news. http://www.theguardian.com/world/2005/jun/10/gender.politicsphilosophyandsociety.

"Arlette Elkaïm-Sartre." *Babelio*. Accessed August 8, 2015. http://www.babelio.com/auteur/Arlette-Elkaim-Sartre/59219.

"Arlette Elkaïm-Sartre (1/5) - Littérature - France Culture." Accessed August 8, 2015. http://www.franceculture.fr/emission-a-voix-nue-arlette-elkaim-sartre-15-2013-06-03.

Aronson, Ronald, and Adrian Van Den Hoven, eds. In *Sartre Alive*. Detroit: Wayne State University Press, 1991.

Bair, Deirdre. *Simone de Beauvoir: A Biography*. Simon and Schuster, 1991.

Benewick, Robert, and Philip Green. *The Routledge Dictionary of Twentieth-Century Political Thinkers*. Routledge, 2002.

Boulé, Jean-Pierre. *Sartre, Self-Formation, and Masculinities*. Berghahn Books, 2005.

Busch, Thomas W. "The Philosophy of Jean-Paul Sartre." Class Lecture, Villanova University, Spring 2014.

Campbell, W. John, and Jean-Paul Sartre. *No Exit and The Flies Notes*. John Wiley & Sons, 1983.

Catalano, Joseph S. *Good Faith and Other Essays: Perspectives on a Sartrean Ethics*. Rowman & Littlefield, 1996.

Catros, Philippe. "Annie Crépin, Histoire de la conscription." *Annales historiques de la Révolution française*, no. 362 (December 1, 2010): 179–80.

CliffsNotes on Sartre's No Exit & The Flies. Lincoln, Neb.: Cliffs Notes, 1983.

Cline, Austin. "Karl Marx on Religion: The Opiate of the Masses?" *About.com Religion & Spirituality*. Accessed December 9, 2015. http://atheism.about.com/od/weeklyquotes/a/marx01.htm.

"Contemporary Philosophy." *Wikipedia, the Free Encyclopedia*, May 21, 2015. https://en.wikipedia.org/w/index.php?title=Contemporary_philosophy&oldid=663373229.

Cox, Gary. *Sartre and Fiction*. A&C Black, 2009.

Darwall, Stephen. *Philosophical Ethics*. Westview Press, 1998.

"Deduction & Induction." Accessed December 17, 2015. http://www.socialresearchmethods.net/kb/dedind.php.

Deguy, Jacques. *Sartre: une écriture critique*. Presses Univ. Septentrion, 2010.

Detmer, David. "Review." *Sartre Studies International* 10, no. 2 (January 1, 2004): 211–15.

Detmer, David J. "Freedom as a Value: A Critique of the Ethical Theory of Jean-Paul Sartre (Existentialism)." Northwestern University, 1986.

Dewey, John. *The Child and the Curriculum*. Martino Fine Books, 2011.

Dobson, Andrew. *Jean-Paul Sartre and the Politics of Reason: A Theory of History*. Cambridge University Press, 1993.

Drake, David. "Sartre, Camus and the Algerian War." *Sartre Studies International* 5, no. 1 (1999): 16–32.

Engel, Patrick. "Negativistic Ethics in Sartre." *Sartre Studies International* 19, no. 1 (June 1, 2013): 16. doi:10.3167/ssi.2013.190102.

"Existential Ethics." Accessed July 26, 2015. http://philosophy.lander.edu/intro/sartre.html.

"Fall of France." *History*. Accessed July 22, 2015. http://www.history.co.uk/study-topics/history-of-ww2/fall-of-france.

Fieser, James. "Ethics | Internet Encyclopedia of Philosophy." Accessed August 7, 2015. http://www.iep.utm.edu/ethics/.

Flynn, Thomas R. *Sartre: A Philosophical Biography*. Cambridge: Cambridge University Press, 2014.

———. *Sartre: A Philosophical Biography*. Cambridge University Press, 2014.

Fraser, Mariam. *Identity Without Selfhood: Simone de Beauvoir and Bisexuality*. Cambridge University Press, 1999.

Fullbrook, Kate, and Edward Fullbrook. *Simone de Beauvoir and Jean-Paul Sartre: The Remaking of a Twentieth-Century Legend*. Harvester Wheatsheaf, 1993.

Fulton, Ann. *Apostles of Sartre: Existentialism in America, 1945-1963*. 1 edition. Evanston, Ill: Northwestern University Press, 1999.

Gerassi, John, ed. *Talking with Sartre: Conversations and Debates*. First Edition. New Haven, CT: Yale University Press, 2009.

Giles, James. *French Existentialism: Consciousness, Ethics, and Relations with Others*. Rodopi, 1999.

Gilligan, Carol. *In a Different Voice: Psychological Theory and Women's Development*. Cambridge, Mass: Harvard University Press, 1998.

Heter, T. Storm. *Sartre's Ethics of Engagement*. A&C Black, 2009.

Hoven, Adrian Van den, and Andrew N. Leak. *Sartre Today: A Centenary Celebration*. Berghahn Books, 2005.

Johnson, Douglas. "A Born-Again Writer." *The Guardian*, October 30, 1987. http://www.theguardian.com/books/1987/oct/30/biography.

Judaken, Jonathan. *Jean-Paul Sartre and the Jewish Question: Anti-Antisemitism and the Politics of the French Intellectual*. U of Nebraska Press, 2006.

Lanchester, John. "High Style." Magazine. *The New Yorker*, January 6, 2003. http://www.newyorker.com/magazine/2003/01/06/high-style-3.

Lavine, T. Z. *From Socrates to Sartre: The Philosophic Quest*. Random House Publishing Group, 2011.

Linsenbard, Gail Evelyn. *An Investigation of Jean-Paul Sartre's Posthumously Published Notebooks for an Ethics*. Edwin Mellen Press, 2000.

Lloyd, Rosemary, and Jean Fornasiero. *Magnificent Obsessions: Honouring the Lives of Hazel Rowley*. Cambridge Scholars Publishing, 2014.

Mann, Anika. "Sartre's Ethics of the Oppressed." *Philosophy Today* 49 (January 1, 2005): 105.

Marx, Karl. *Marxism, Socialism and Religion*. Resistance Books, 2001.

McBride, William Leon, and Calvin O. Schrag. *Phenomenology in a Pluralistic Context*. SUNY Press, 1983.

McEwen, Todd, and Lucy Ellmann. "Damp Squibs." *The Guardian*, January 14, 2006, sec. Books. http://www.theguardian.com/books/2006/jan/14/highereducation.biography.

Merriam-Webster's Desk Dictionary. 1 edition. Springfield, Mass: Merriam-Webster, 1995.

Meszaros, Istvan. *The Work of Sartre*. New York: Monthly Review Press, 2012.

"Metaethics | Define Metaethics at Dictionary.com." Accessed August 7, 2015. http://dictionary.reference.com/browse/metaethics.

"Nobel Prize in Literature 1964 - Press Release." Accessed August 8, 2015. http://www.nobelprize.org/nobel_prizes/literature/laureates/1964/press.html.

O'Neil, Patrick M. *Great World Writers: Twentieth Century*. Marshall Cavendish, 2004.

Pace, Edward Aloysius, and James Hugh Ryan. *The New Scholasticism*. American Catholic Philosophical Association, 1970.

Petersen, Thomas Søbirk, Jesper Ryberg, Thomas Søbirk Petersen, and Jesper Ryberg. "Applied Ethics," May 10, 2010. http://www.oxfordbibliographies.com/display/id/obo-9780195396577-0006.

Poster, Mark. *Existential Marxism in Postwar France: From Sartre to Althusser*. First Edition Thus edition. Princeton, N.J: Princeton University Press, 1976.

Pramaggiore, Maria, and Donald E. Hall. *RePresenting Bisexualities: Subjects and Cultures of Fluid Desire*. NYU Press, 1996.

Priest, Stephen. *The Subject in Question: Sartre's Critique of Husserl in The Transcendence of the Ego*. Routledge, 2002.

Ranwez, Alain D. *Jean-Paul Sartre's Les Temps Modernes, a Literary History, 1945-1952*. Whitston Pub. Co., 1981.

Rau, Catherine. "The Ethical Theory of Jean-Paul Sartre." *The Journal of Philosophy* 46, no. 17 (August 18, 1949): 536–45.

Rest, James R., and Darcia Narvez. *Moral Development in the Professions: Psychology and Applied Ethics*. Psychology Press, 1994.

"Revue Les Temps Modernes - Gallimard - Site Gallimard."

Accessed August 8, 2015.
http://www.gallimard.fr/Catalogue/GALLIMARD/Revue-Les-Temps-Modernes.

Rowley, Hazel. *Tête-a-Tête: The Tumultuous Lives and Loves of Simone de Beauvoir and Jean-Paul Sartre*. New York: Harper Perennial, 2006.

Sabbaghi, Rachid. "Sartre." *UNESCO Courier*, September 1, 1992, 31.

Sartre, Jean-Paul. *Search for a Method*. New York: Vintage, 1968.

———. *The Philosophy of Jean-Paul Sartre*. Vintage Books edition. New York: Vintage, 2003.

———. *The Words: The Autobiography of Jean-Paul Sartre*. First Edition. Braziller, 1964.

———. *Les Mots*. 1St Edition. Librairie Gallimard, 1964.

Seel, Gerhard. "La morale de Sartre. Une reconstruction." *Le Portique. Revue de philosophie et de sciences humaines*, no. 16 (September 1, 2005).
https://leportique.revues.org/737?lang=en.

Simont, Juliette. *Ecrits posthumes de Sartre, II: avec un inédit de Jean-Paul Sartre*. Vrin, 2001.

Stone, Bob, and Elizabeth Bowman. *Ethique Dialectique: Un premier regard aux notes de la conference de Rome, 1964*. Editions de l'Universite de Bruxelles. Brussels: Editions de l'Universite de Bruxelles, 1987.

Sumner, Leonard Wayne. "Normative Ethics and Metaethics." *Ethics* 77, no. 2 (January 1, 1967): 95–106.

Thomas, Busch W. "Thomas W." Accessed August 8, 2015. http://www22.homepage.villanova.edu/thomas.busch/.

Tymieniecka, Anna-Teresa. *Husserlian Phenomenology in a New Key: Intersubjectivity, Ethos, the Societal Sphere, Human Encounter, Pathos Book 2 Phenomenology in the World Fifty Years after the Death of Edmund Husserl*. Springer Science & Business Media, 2012.

Velasquez, Manuel, Claire Andre, Thomas Shanks, S. J., and Michael J. Meyer. "What Is Ethics?," Fall 1987. http://www.scu.edu/ethics/practicing/decision/whatisethics.html.

Warburton, Nigel. "A Student's Guide to Jean-Paul Sartre's Existentialism and Humanism | Issue 15 | Philosophy Now." Accessed July 17, 2015. https://philosophynow.org/issues/15/A_students_guide_to_Jean-Paul_Sartres_Existentialism_and_Humanism.

"What Is Systematic Approach? Definition and Meaning." Accessed December 17, 2015. http://www.investorwords.com/19342/systematic_approach.html.

"When Sartre Talked to Crabs (It Was Mescaline)." *The New York Times*, November 15, 2009, sec. Week in Review. http://www.nytimes.com/2009/11/15/weekinreview/15grist.htm.

Zheng, Yiwei. *Ontology and Ethics in Sartre's Early Philosophy*. Lexington Books, 2005.

Bibliography

Acknowledgments

I started dotting the first lines for this book as a class project. As a graduate student in Political Science, I attended a course about Jean-Paul Sartre. The course was taught by Thomas Busch. Dr. Busch is a well-known professor of Philosophy at Villanova University.[7] He is a distinguished Sartrean scholar.

Dr. Busch is well vested in Sartrean Philosophy. He published several essays about Sartre. He has an extensive background in Sartrean philosophy.[8]

I learned a lot from Dr. Busch's expertise. I learned a lot about Sartre. It was a wonderful learning experience. The course is among the highlights of my education.

Dr. Busch examined the life and the philosophy of Jean-Paul Sartre. It was a privilege to have the opportunity to learn about Sartre from a well-respected scholar. The course changed my

---

[7] Thomas W. Busch is a Professor at Villanova University (Department of Philosophy). His research interests center on French Phenomenology and Existentialism.

[8] Busch W. Thomas, "Thomas W," accessed August 8, 2015, http://www22.homepage.villanova.edu/thomas.busch/.

ACKNOWLEDGMENTS

perspectives about this great thinker. The present work was designed to reflect that view.

During my academic experience, I learned about a side about Jean-Paul Sartre, which I never knew. Thanks to Dr. Busch, I learned a lot about Sartrean ethics, though I am not suggesting that Dr. Busch shares the views I expressed about Sartre throughout the text. It is irrefutable that Dr. Busch's course inspired me to compile this book.

I would like to extend my gratitude to Dr. Busch. His insights helped me understand Jean-Paul Sartre better. Thanks to his expertise, I learned to develop a practical approach to examine the crux of Sartrean philosophy.

As the name of the title suggests, this book is in defense of Jean-Paul Sartre. As should be apparent by now [if you read the manuscript cover-to-cover], this work does not delve in detail in the Sartrean approach to various philosophical principles. The focus was on Sartre's literary portfolio about ethics.

Whether you are an avid reader of Sartrean philosophy, this work was concocted to help you understand Jean-Paul Sartre. Although this is not an in-depth examination of Sartre's literary achievements, it is relevant. I hope that you were able to immerse yourself in the manuscript. I hope that you learned a lot from it.

December 6, 2016
Ben Wood Johnson, Ph.D.

Updated April 2021

INDEX

* E-Book does not contain an index.

Abandon, 27, 29, 37–39, 45–46, 91, 128, 158, 175
Absolute, 123
Abstract, 8, 22, 54, 72, 131, 145–146, 173
 Abstract concepts, 8
 Abstract idealistic, 131
 Abstraction, 100, 145–146
Academic, 3, 149, 175, 177, 180
 Academic civility, 149
 Academic journals, 177, 180
Achieve, 46, 149
Achievements, 44, 120, 128, 130–131, 133, 147
Active, [also see: Sartre]
 Active in ethics, 61
Adhere, 72, 118
Admirers, 75
Adopted, [also see: Arlette]

Adoptive daughter, [also see: Elkaïm]
Adrian, [also see: Hoven Adrian Van Den]
Affair, 55
 Affair of the individual, 55
Affect, 67, 120, 149, 151
Agency, 83, 120
 Agency of the individual, 83
 Agent, [also see: Moral]
Age-old question, 173
Alienation, 148
Allegorical, 12
All-inclusive, 9, 20, 69, 83–84, 125
Ambiguous, 128
Analyze, 10, 39, 47, 82, 121
Anderson Thomas, 1, 3, 13–14, 16, 23, 49, 72, 74, 93–95, 101, 114, 124–125, 128–130, 133, 137–139, 141–150, 153, 156–159
Anguish, 25–26

Anti-Sartrean, 73
Anti-Semite, 110, 113
AntiSemitism, 110
Appendices, 3, 177
Aquinas Thomas, 90
Arbitrary, 30, 43
Archaic, 173
Area, 106
 Area of philosophy, 106
Argumentative, 11–12
 Argumentative structure, 11
Aristotle, 43, 90
Aronson Ronald, 1, 40, 45, 48–49
Articulate, 76, 86
Assumption, 2, 39, 41, 49, 82, 106, 112, 118
Attention, 17, 133
Attitude, 26, 55, 81, 91, 149
Augustine of hippo, 90
Authority, 61, 92, 151
Avid, 45, 112, 122, 131
 Avid critics, 45
 Avid opponents, 112

INDEX

Aware, 25, 37, 110, 112–113, 121–122, 158
Aware of their environment, 112
Aware of the self, 122, 158
Bad, 26, 96, 123, 147, 157–158
Bad faith, 26, 90, 123, 147, 157–158
Balance, 15, 42, 45, 56, 85, 146
Bankrupt, 109
Baseless, 78
Basis, 58, 62, 123
Basis for oppression, 123
Being, 9–10, 23–26, 31, 44, 46–47, 55–56, 59, 62, 66, 72, 78, 83–85, 87, 89, 91, 99, 101, 106–108, 118–124, 129, 132, 139, 145–146, 148–150, 157–158, 166
Being-for-itself, [also see: Being - Being-in-and-for-itself]
Being-in-and-for-itself, 121–122, 131
Being-in-a-pair-with-the-other, [also see: Being - Being-in-and-for-itself]
Being-in-itself, [also see: Being - Being-in-the-midst-of-the-world]
Being-in-the-midst-of-the-world, 119, 121
Being-objects, [also see: Being-for-others]
Being-with-others, 123
Being-for-others, 122–123
Being-for-other, 123
Belief, 8, 13, 22, 41, 90, 164
Bentham Jeremy, 43
Bernstein Richard, [also see: Commentators]
Bibliography, 3
Biography, 179
Blunder, 107

Body, 14, 42, 79, 118, 153
Body of materials, 14
Bowman Elizabeth, 1, 3, 12–14, 16, 23, 74, 94–95, 101–102, 125, 128–129, 133–138, 151, 154–157, 159
Brilliant philosopher, 144
Broad concept, 40
Brutal, 75
Build-up, 123
Burst out, 120
Busch, 15, 176
Cahiers, 10–11, 38, 46, 48–49, 67, 90
Cahiers pour une morale, 10–11, 38, 46, 48–49, 67, 90
Career, 10, 46, 61, 75–76, 78, 81–82, 87, 118, 120, 131, 141, 157–158, 174
Catalog, 43, 95
Categorical, 136, 154
Categorical duties, 136
Caution, 21
Centerpiece, 59
Centrality, 41
Challenge, 12, 57–58, 61
Characteristic, 20, 85, 119, 131, 135, 145, 158
Chasm, 47
Chimerical, 90, 123
Choice, 46, 119, 124, 147, 154–155
Circle, 40, 54, 60, 154
Circular, 14
Circumstance, 55, 173
Civil, 158
Civility, 149, 175
Clarify, 56, 120
Clarity, 112, 145
Clear-cut, 73
Close, 91, 97
Clue, 146
Co-dependency, 120
Cogency, 11, 65
Coherence, 93
Coherent, 41, 81, 94, 110, 173

Coincide, 147, 155
Collapse, 119
Collection, 11–13, 20, 44, 78, 81, 87, 91, 94, 111–112, 129
Collective, 158
Collective freedom, 158
Collective needs, 158
Combative, 2
Commitment, 21
Commonsense, 141
Commonsensical, 83, 143
Communicated, 175
Communism, 158
Community, 55, 67, 85, 103, 107, 115, 124, 139
Compensate, 11
Compilation, 3, 20, 23, 29, 33, 37, 40, 49, 58, 64, 72, 75, 79, 92–94, 98, 165
Complaints, 100
Complication, 83
Component, 44
Comprehensive, 21, 95, 113
Compromise, 66
Compulsion, 145, 156
Concede, 11, 76, 137
Conceivable, 56, 154
Concept, 8, 39–40, 47, 54–55, 62, 64–65, 67, 72, 83, 85, 87, 99, 142, 163, 165
Conception, 66, 146
Conceptual, 77
Concern, 11, 24, 30, 37, 46, 54–56, 62, 64, 74, 78–79, 84, 90–91, 93–94, 106, 109, 111, 115, 117–118, 120, 131–132, 149, 158, 164, 167
Concerning, 40, 94
Concession, 38, 66, 84
Conciliatory, 12
Concrete, 54, 119, 131, 145–146, 153
Concrete reality, 145

202

Concrete relations, 119
Concrete understandings, 54
Concretize, 45, 47, 90, 108
Condition, 55, 115, 142–143, 168
Conditional, 147
Conduct, 15, 20, 55, 57, 59, 66, 83, 103, 109, 111–112, 121, 132, 134–137, 142–143, 147, 156, 166
Confident, 38–39, 67
Conflict, 72–73, 75, 99, 122, 147
Conform, 156
Connection, 106, 112, 117, 134, 139
Conscience, 121
Conscious, 25, 148
Consciousness, 122–123, 145–148, 153, 156, 158
Consensus, 29, 40
Consequentialism, 108
Consideration, 10, 15, 20, 27, 45, 66, 71, 74, 80, 82, 85, 93, 99, 106, 112, 131–133, 147, 164–165
Consistent, 30, 40–41, 91, 93
Constituent, 1, 111, 128
Constrained, 121
Constraints, 120, 155
Contemplate, 26
Contemplation, 165
Contemporary, 2, 36, 67, 113, 135, 163
Contention, 28, 44, 56, 65–66, 81
Contentious, 44, 78, 106
Context, 15, 54, 75, 83, 98, 113, 122, 134, 150
Contextual, 77
Continue, 35, 48, 62
Contradict, 22, 157
Contradiction, 99, 124
Contradictory, 63, 121, 164

Contrary, 54, 63, 80, 92, 99–100, 106, 166, 173
Contribution, 5, 8, 10, 20, 22, 24, 35, 40–43, 47, 56, 59, 81–82, 89, 100, 106, 112, 163–164, 179
Contributor, 21, 39–40, 76, 132, 164–165
Controversial, 2, 42, 71
Controversies, 44, 100
Convert, 60
Conviction, 21, 73, 130
Conviviality, 148–149
Cornell, 16, 96–98, 101–102, 129, 135, 137–138, 159
Cornell university, 97–98, 129, 135
Cornerstone, 149
Correlation, 141
Counterproductive, 82
Creative, 57
Credence, 150
Credenda, 71
Credit, 39, 84, 132, 164
Criticism, 2–3, 5, 9, 13–14, 17, 19–23, 28, 30–31, 33, 39, 44–45, 56, 59–60, 65, 74–76, 81–82, 90–92, 99, 110, 112–113, 127, 130, 133, 148, 161, 165, 175
Critique, 55, 82, 87, 89
Misplaced, 20
Ulterior motive, 36
Crucial, 56, 92
Crux, 5, 9, 21, 25, 56, 69, 82, 107, 113
Culture, 2, 113, 164
Cumbersome, 40
Curiosity, 100
Current, 9, 27, 36, 39, 45, 48, 51, 75, 91–92, 100, 105, 132, 149, 175
Customs, 156
Cynical, 30
Cynicism, 21
Deal, 94

De Beauvoir Simone, 177
Decision, 37, 39, 155
Decompression, 121
Dedicate, 17, 24, 46, 56, 86
Deepen, 120
Defender, 92
Defensible, 111
Definite, 174
Définitif, 37
Definition, 30
Definitive, 20, 106
Dégénère, 180
Degradation, 148
Deliberation, 124
Deliver, 98, 129, 131, 135
Deny, 27, 30, 61, 63, 91, 93, 100, 106–108, 111, 120, 128–129, 137, 166–167
Deny sartre, 27, 30, 91
Deny sartrean ethics, 93
Deontology, 54, 108
Departure, 12, 48
Dependence, 154
Depict, 75, 98, 100
Deprivation, 62
Depriving, 10, 61
Describe, 1, 23, 84, 133, 144
Descriptive, 133
Descriptors, 55
Deserve, 74, 77, 79, 118
Desire, 80, 119, 147–148, 158
Desperate, 39
Despite, 2, 13, 38, 48, 54, 58, 66, 73, 84, 90, 92, 100, 124, 127, 130, 132, 149, 155, 165–166
Destiny, 121, 147, 154
Destructive, 3, 44
Detach, 58, 130, 146
Detail, 15, 36, 120, 130, 142
Determination, 93, 130, 154–155
Detmer, 2, 31, 48, 113

Index

Develop, 10–12, 30, 38, 49, 56, 62, 64, 66, 76, 87, 90–91, 93, 99, 109, 112, 118, 132–133, 157, 164–166, 168
Développées, 38
Developing, 38
Device, 38
Devient, 46
Devote, 27, 90
Dialectical, 87, 89, 91, 156
Dialectical reason, 87, 89
Dialectical sense, 156
Dimension, 78
Diplomatic, 128
Direction, 28, 42, 46, 98, 141, 154
Disagree, 8, 10, 12, 22, 28–29, 63–64, 73, 79, 99, 110, 133, 147, 164
Disagreements, 30, 48, 72–73, 149
Disapproval, 128, 156
Discarded, 37
Discipline, 1, 8–10, 13–15, 20–22, 25, 30, 39–40, 61, 71, 73, 75–76, 80–81, 84, 91, 94, 109, 112, 127, 130, 132–133, 161, 164, 166, 175, 179
Discourse, 9, 28, 36, 39, 48, 72, 80, 86, 91, 105, 149
Discover, 29, 85, 123, 133, 167
Discuss, 13, 15, 17, 54, 63, 74, 85, 87, 90, 99–100, 151
Discussion, 12–13, 23, 60, 129, 137, 171
Disentangle, 22, 26, 46, 108
Dishonest, 82
Disinclination, 127
Disjointed, 20, 41, 64, 80, 93, 98, 112, 127, 132–133
Dismiss, 23, 76, 90, 105, 118, 131

Disparaging, 51
Disparagements, 92
Dispossession, 62
Disputation, 30, 166
Dispute, 14, 22, 35, 41, 47, 54, 65, 75–76, 98, 112, 133, 139
Disqualify, 78
Dissected, 76, 92
Dissension, 76
Dissent, 10
Dissenters, 165
Dissenting, 15, 28, 76, 82
Dissociate, 26
Distance, 26, 147
Distention, 107
Distillate, 94
Distinct, 3, 46, 62, 66, 108, 121
Distinction, 48, 93, 99, 110, 145
Distinctively, 168
Distinctly, 47, 95, 98
Distinguish, 110, 121, 123
Distractions, 2
Disunity, 72
Diverge, 60
Divergence, 79
Diverging, 69
Diverse, 72
Doctrine, 89
Doubt, 35, 54, 74, 93, 99–100, 143, 163
Doubtful, 30
Drawback, 10, 74
Dualism, 134
Dubious, 108
Duty, 21, 24, 74, 103, 111–112, 136, 154, 156
Eager, 57
Early, 59–61, 93–94, 120, 125, 129, 139, 141, 149, 151, 156–158
Economic, 121
Economies, 154
Effect, 37, 39, 121–122, 124, 168
Effective, 136, 154
Efficacy, 135

Effort, 3, 15, 42, 72–73, 90, 108, 110, 123
Ego, 91, 99, 142
Egocentric, 111
Egoism, 168
Elaboration, 81
Element, 29, 91, 110, 153, 155
Eligible, 164
Elkaïm, 8, 16
Elkaïm-Sartre Arlette, [also see: Elkaïm-Sartre Arlette - Daughter]
Daughter, 8–11, 20, 37, 48, 58, 69, 80, 83, 96
Elusive, 49, 84, 107, 128, 131, 137, 165
Emanate, 20, 72, 79, 82, 108, 134–135
Embedded, 131
Embodied, 91
Embrace, 60, 132, 158
Embryonic, 13, 111, 125
Emotion, 31, 146–147, 150, 167–169
Emotionally, 168
Empirical, 3, 25, 123
Empty, 64, 147
Encourage, 48, 156
Engage, 55, 75, 91, 107, 155–156
Engage in conducts, 55
Engaging, 86
English, 90
Engrained, 134
Enlighten, 129
Entity, 26, 59, 157, 174
Entrenched, 27, 47, 95, 99, 141
Epistemological, 175
Epitome, 58
Epochs, 72
Erroneous, 49
Error, 30, 63, 81, 100, 164
Escape, 26, 119
Essays, 7, 11, 13, 20–21, 24, 27, 37, 59–60, 78, 81, 85, 90–91, 111–

204

113, 128, 132, 158, 174
Essence, 9, 22, 27, 47, 58, 65, 76, 78, 81–82, 100, 106, 112, 148, 168
Essential, 109
Essentiality, 75, 136
Essentially, 157
Esteem, 73
Eternal, 99
Etiology, 110, 113
Être et le néant, 129
Etymon, 65
Evaluate, 5, 43–44, 48, 54–55, 58–59, 115, 135–136, 151, 166
Event, 37, 44
Evidence, 12, 57, 61, 63, 66, 76, 80, 82, 173
Evoke, 11, 43, 54, 56, 62, 65, 112, 120, 123, 125, 168
Evoking, 42, 155
Evolve, 55
Evolution, 135, 142, 146
Exaggerated, 2, 8, 93, 145
Exaggeration, 1
Examination, 20–21, 30, 47–48, 59, 62, 77, 79–80, 84–85, 90, 94, 109, 118, 125, 128, 134, 144, 151, 165–168
Exclusive, 75
Exhaustive, 3, 11, 97, 173, 180
Exhibit, 29
Exhibition, 84, 146
Exist, 13, 15, 25, 41, 54, 60–61, 64, 72, 74, 79–80, 98, 107, 113, 118, 123, 125, 129–130, 133, 135, 149, 168, 174
Existence, 20, 76, 89, 94, 100–101, 106–108, 120–122, 163, 166, 168, 173
Existent, 26

Existentialist, 47, 59, 62, 66, 109–110, 165, 174
Existential, 25, 148, 168
Existentialism, 3, 30–31, 38, 45–46, 58–59, 62–63, 82, 89, 99, 109, 113, 118, 129–130, 134, 139, 150–151, 160, 165–169, 173–174
Existentially, 112
Expedient, 44, 58
Experience, 15, 66, 86, 122–123, 136, 141–143, 145–147, 175–176
Expert, 72, 75, 107, 128, 164
Expertise, 165
Expertly, 176
Explicate, 37, 54, 106, 175
Explicit, 119
Express, 23, 111
Expression, 54
Exquisite, 130
Extensive, 60, 96, 130
Facticity, 119, 123, 147, 153–154
Facto, 148
Factors, 82, 121, 134, 142, 154–155, 157
Failing, 36, 77
Failure, 13, 22, 29, 38, 63–64, 85, 108, 118, 120–121, 130, 149, 156, 158
Fair, 80, 109, 113, 149
Faire, 37
Faith, [also see: Bad - Bad faith]
Fall, 72, 91, 123
Familiar, 59, 76, 128
Famous, 43, 59, 75, 90, 110
Fame, 2, 130

Fanatical, [also see: Sartrean - Defend - Defense]
Farce, 131
Farfetched, 60, 90, 143
Favor, 3, 14, 23, 69, 132, 148, 171
Fear, 147
Feasible, 61, 107
Feature, 3, 10, 12, 59, 87, 97, 117, 129, 135, 168, 177, 179
Fecundity, 73, 86
Feeble, 93
Feel, 66, 122, 147
Fell, 28, 36, 65, 129, 149
Figure, 42, 75–77, 95–96, 98, 143–144
Final, 3, 15, 106
Finitude, 123
Fissure, 61, 73
Fixed, 158
Fixing, 135
Flagrant, 42
Flaubert, 91
Flaws, 28, 64, 112, 179
Flow, 11
Flynn Thomas, 1, 102, 179
Focus, 1, 5, 29, 44, 46, 51, 59, 69, 75, 82, 86, 129, 139, 151, 179
Follow, 24, 131
Footing, 106
Forces, 154
Forging, 103, 115
For-itself, 25, 119, 121, 123, 148
Formulate, 167
Formule, 37
Foundation, 8, 11, 15, 20–21, 25, 30, 42, 59, 61–62, 64, 66, 77, 79–80, 87, 94, 98, 103, 109, 113, 117–118, 129–130, 135, 137, 141, 143–145, 147, 158, 165, 167
Founding, 64

205

Fragments, 10, 13–14, 35–37, 41, 60, 77, 95, 125, 132
Frame, 20, 109–110, 130, 174
Framework, 10
France, 16
Free, 25, 110–112, 119–120, 124, 147, 154, 157
Freedom, 1, 9, 25–27, 46–48, 55, 66, 74, 85, 90, 98–103, 106, 110–111, 113, 115, 118–124, 131–132, 137, 142–144, 146–149, 151, 153–155, 157–158, 174
French, 54, 67, 90
Function, 137, 158
Fundamental, 26, 67, 81, 92, 121, 123, 131, 133, 142, 157, 163
Fusion, 25
Fustigate, 9, 20, 23
Futility, 15, 30
Future, 17, 24, 27, 37, 46, 56, 90, 94, 154
Gain, 39, 58, 115, 119–120, 149
Gap, 59, 127, 129
Gauge, 30
Gauging, 11
Gaze, 45
Gelassenheit, 72
Genie, 179–180
Genuine, 13, 24, 48, 72, 99, 109–110, 113, 118
Giant, 71, 74
Gist, 28, 33, 45, 48, 56, 60, 65, 75, 79, 106
Glimpse, 20, 129
Glitch, 168
Glory, 20, 166
God, 149, 168
Govern, 55, 149
Gramsci, 98
Grandiose, 82
Grapple, 175

Grasp, 8, 25, 44, 56, 69, 84, 92, 112, 118, 125, 129, 133, 145, 157, 175
Grasping, 62, 100, 109, 135
Groundwork, 9, 109
Growth, 174
Guide, 39, 112, 121, 137, 144, 155
Guru, 80
Hallmarks, 69
Handwritten, 11, 24, 95–97
Haphazardly, 59
Hate, 110, 113, 122–123, 154
Head-on, 10
Heart of Sartrean ethics, 139
Hegelian lens, 111
Heidegger, 86
Heter, 2, 113–114
Hippo, 90
Historic, 155
Historical, 121, 136, 142, 155
History, 3, 16, 72, 93, 95–97, 101–102, 137–138, 142, 155, 159
Hobbes Thomas, 90
Holistic, 77, 83
All-inclusive approach, 9, 83–84
All-of-the-above, 83
Holistically, 44, 49
Honor, 24, 27, 29, 90
Household, 71
Hoven Adrian Van Den, 1, 40, 45, 48–49
Hubris, 39
Human, 1, 3, 9, 11–12, 20, 26, 30–31, 37, 39–40, 44, 46–47, 54–55, 58, 61–63, 66, 72, 76, 78, 83, 89–90, 99, 101, 103, 106, 109–110, 113, 119–121, 130, 132, 134–135, 137, 139, 142–143, 145–

151, 153–154, 156–158, 161, 163, 165–169, 173–175, 179
Humanisme, 47
Humanistic, 123, 142
Humanity, 59
Hunches, 135
Hyperbole, 1
Hyperbolic, 133, 144
Hypocritical, 107
Hypothesis, 49
Hypothetical, 136
Hysteria, 1
Ideal, [also see: Idealistic]
Idealistic, 106, 123, 131, 143–144, 168
Ideals, 118, 142, 155–157
Identity, 9–10, 12, 28, 41, 73, 115, 119, 121, 128, 157–158
Ill-conceived, 173, 175
Imagination, 47
Immersed, [also see: Individual]
Impact, 14, 22, 56, 60, 106, 173
Impetus, 40
Implication, 63, 67, 90, 148–149, 155, 168, 174
Imprint, 2–3, 8, 90
Imprudent, 109
Inachevés, 37
Inauthentic, 36
Inauthenticity, 110
Incapable, 26–27, 133
Incite, 2, 24–25, 40
Inclination, 136
Incompleteness, 38
Incomprehensible, 38
Inconceivable, 98
Inconclusive, 8
Incongruent, 22, 74, 79, 125, 131
Incongruity, 22, 98
Inconsequential, 38, 42, 57, 133
Inconsistency, 11, 30, 45
Independent, 46, 86, 158, 174

Indiscriminate, 10, 118
Individual, 26, 46–47, 55, 59, 64, 66–67, 82–83, 85, 90, 98–99, 103, 107, 110–112, 115, 117, 119–124, 130–132, 134–137, 139, 142–143, 147–149, 151, 153–158, 165–168, 174
  Act, 49, 55, 86, 112, 119, 121, 123–124, 130, 134, 137, 139, 145–147, 154–157
  Authentic, 24, 49, 59, 98–99, 103, 110, 112–114
  Individualism, 168
  Individually, 26, 134
Induce, 92
  Induction, 48
  Inductive, 43–44, 48–49
  Inductively, 43–44
Inert, 146
Inescapable, 168
Inevitably, 148
Inextricably, 19, 100, 121, 167
Influence, 124, 137, 143, 158, 163–164
In-itself, 25, 119, 121
In-itself-for-itself, 26
Injustice, 55
Inquirer, 41–42, 44, 49, 75, 81, 85–86, 94
Inquiry, 15, 23, 41–42, 85, 109
Inquisitive, 174
Insights, 58, 74, 80, 174–175
Institutions, 134, 156
Instrumentality, 8
Instrumentation, 11
Integral, 59, 62, 82
Intentional, 139, 145–147
  Intentionally, 8, 77
Interiority, 157
Internal, 135
Internalize, 130
Interplay, 130

Interpretation, 43, 66, 78, 92, 135, 142, 175
Interview, 10, 16
Intimate, 59, 76, 145, 157
Intimated, 48, 105, 131
Intransigence, 166
Intrinsic, 46, 118, 120, 139, 148–149, 157
Introduce, 75, 177
Introductory, 10, 179
Introspection, 59
  Introspective, 85, 134
Investigation, 3, 29, 31, 44, 57, 133
  Investigative, 57
Irrelevance, 175
Irrelevant, 73, 100, 112, 132
Irresponsible, 64
Jew, 110, 113
Journals, 177, 180
Justice, 55
Justification, 111
Justify, 40, 74
Kant Emmanuel, 90
  Kantian duties, 111
Killing, 111
Kind, 72, 165
Knowledge, 82, 102
Labor, 12, 86
Lack, 10–11, 20, 23, 26, 28, 30, 38, 41–42, 47, 63, 78–80, 85, 110, 118, 121, 145, 149, 157, 161, 168
Languages, 156
Laughable, 36
Law, 156
Lecteur, 38
Lecture, 13, 16, 78, 94–98, 101–102, 129–130, 135, 137–138, 159
Legacy, 1–3, 23, 29, 45, 55, 74, 100, 106, 108, 175, 179
Legendary, 87
Legitimacy, 43, 92
Liberal, 111
Library, 58, 91
License, 27, 38, 111

Life, 45, 141, 143, 149, 154, 156
  Lifestyles, 111
  Lifetime, 7, 24, 93, 131
Like, 29, 43, 45, 72, 90, 92, 106, 111, 119, 143, 145, 158
  Likelihood, 24, 108, 110, 131
  Likely, 12, 24, 42, 72, 79, 83, 106, 117, 131
  Likeness, 130
Limit, 48, 51, 57–58, 83, 154–155
Literary, 1–3, 7–9, 12–14, 20, 22–24, 28–29, 35–36, 38–40, 43–44, 54, 58, 60–61, 64, 67, 71–74, 76–77, 80–85, 87, 90–91, 94–95, 100, 105–106, 112, 118, 120, 127–128, 130–133, 141, 147–148, 163, 165, 174, 179–180
Literature, 2, 5, 10, 12–13, 15, 20, 22–23, 27, 29–31, 36, 39–40, 42, 45, 48–49, 57, 59–60, 62, 64–65, 69, 72–73, 75, 78, 81, 86, 89, 92–94, 108, 110, 113, 127, 133–134, 139, 163–164, 166, 179
Locke John, 43, 90
Logic, 91, 111–112, 127
Logistical, 57
Long-winded, 27
L'Existentialisme, 47
Magazines, 177, 180
Magisterial, 110
Magnum, 71
Majestic, 129
Malleable, 40
Man, 2, 25, 29, 39, 42–43, 45, 59, 61, 82, 84, 112, 121, 146–147, 168, 175

Index

Manuscript, 3–4, 9, 13, 23–24, 29, 36, 39, 41, 44, 78, 90, 96–98, 179
Marcel Gabriel, 90
Maritain Jacques, 90
Marxist perspective, 123
Maturation, 93
Mazis, 176
Media, 155
Merit, 2, 43, 47, 66, 74, 79–80, 84, 93, 106, 112, 127–128, 164, 167
Metaethical, 108
Metamorphic, 141
Metaphysical, 46
Method, 5, 21, 30–31, 118, 133, 136
Methodical, 20–21, 57, 115
Meticulous, 20
Meticulously, 92, 117
Mill John Stuart, 90
Mindset, 109, 129
Minor, 36
Minority, 15, 164, 166, 175
Misguided, 11, 33, 38, 41, 78–81, 94, 113, 120, 164
Misinformed, 165
Misinterpretations, 73
Misjudgments, 110, 165
Misleading, 147
Misnomer, 109
Mistaken, 39, 82, 84, 107, 132
Misunderstanding, 110
Mode, 46, 62, 83, 132
Modality, 46, 121
Model, 9, 42, 59, 62–63, 66, 72, 84, 105, 125, 135, 144, 149, 156, 165, 174, 180
Modern, 2, 40, 62, 72
Modestly, 65
Moi, 145
Moral, 1–2, 5, 8–10, 12–14, 19–22, 24–28, 30, 39–42, 44–47, 51, 54, 56, 60, 64, 66, 71–75, 78, 81, 83, 90, 92, 94–97, 100, 103, 105, 108, 110–112, 125, 129–133, 135–136, 143, 149, 155, 157, 164–168, 171, 173
Morale, 10–11, 38, 46, 48–49, 67, 90
Moralist, 54, 90, 166
Moraliste, 54
Moralité, 46
Morality, 1, 3, 5, 11–12, 16, 25–26, 30, 37, 44, 46–47, 54–56, 59, 61–63, 67, 83, 86, 94–97, 101–102, 120, 130–132, 135, 137–138, 143, 159, 161, 166–167
Morally, 55
Mores, 156
Mort, 37
Mots, 37
Museum, 58
Mutual, 111, 120, 156, 161
Mutually, 75
Narrow, 1, 20, 22, 81
Narrow perspective, 20, 81
Narrow understanding, 22
Nature, 1, 5, 8–9, 20, 22, 26–27, 30, 35, 40–41, 43, 48, 60, 62, 73, 78–79, 81, 84, 91, 93–94, 101, 107–108, 112, 119, 121, 128, 130, 132, 136, 142, 154, 166
Natural, 121
Neutral, 12, 15, 23, 41, 59, 74, 128, 179
Neutrality, 80
Newspapers, 177, 180
Niche, 62
Nietzsche Frederick, 90
Non, 10
Non-being, 87, 99, 121, 146
Non-conscious, 146
Non-consciousness, 146
Non-constructive, 23
Nonexistent, 12, 29
Non-issue, 36
No-no, 36
Non-objective, 153
Non-scholars, 165
Nonsense, 72
Normative, 108
Norms, 55, 111, 149, 154–156, 161
Notebooks, 7, 31, 41, 54, 76, 78, 90–92, 94, 98, 101–102, 111, 113–114, 128, 153, 168
Nothingness, 9, 24–26, 31, 46, 56, 59, 78, 87, 89, 101, 118–122, 124, 129, 132, 146, 149–150, 157
Nullify, 38
Obeys, 111
Object-ness, 122
Object, 12, 23, 59, 66, 85, 93, 121–123, 136, 144–148
Objectification, 119, 121, 148
Objectified, 123, 148
Objections, 72
Objective, 12, 75, 108, 122, 146
Objectively, 2, 22, 86
Objectivity, 120–121, 123
Obligated, 157
Obligation, 86
Obscure, 35, 37–38, 66, 72
Observation, 49, 148
Official, 128
Omission, 120
Omnipresent, 82
One-century-per-genie, 180
One-dimensional, 29
Oneself, 157
One-sided, 20, 23, 42, 59
Onslaught, 23
Ontological, 26, 46–47, 62, 82, 99, 106, 123, 136–137, 166

Ontology, 3, 9, 20, 25, 30, 39, 46–47, 54–55, 58–59, 61–63, 66–67, 76, 78, 83, 90, 99–101, 103, 106, 109–110, 113, 121–122, 129, 132, 134–136, 142, 151, 158, 161, 163, 165, 167–168, 174–175
Ontologique, 46
Open-mind, 81
Open-mindedness, 81
Opi, 71, 78
Opinion, 28, 61, 73, 75, 142
Opponents, 22, 74–75, 85, 112, 134, 165
Opposition, 44, 81
Oppression, 123
Optimistic, 84
Origin, 5, 72, 83
Other, 3–4, 7–9, 11–12, 14, 19–24, 28–29, 40–42, 47, 49, 53, 55, 58–63, 66, 74–76, 78, 82, 84–85, 89–90, 92, 94, 96–97, 107–108, 111–114, 117, 119–124, 128–129, 131–135, 147–148, 154, 158, 165–166, 173, 175, 179–180
Other-as-object, 119
Outlook, 95, 120, 143
Outnumber, 23
Outshine, 163
Outside, 72, 145
Overlap, 174
Overlook, 22, 41, 45, 81, 83, 87, 132, 134
Overshadows, 108
Pamphlets, 77
Paradigm, 20, 62, 109
Paradox, 157
Passion, 25, 112, 147
Path, 99, 110, 155
Pedestal, 131
Pellauer, 1, 31, 90–93, 99–100, 106–108

Perceive, 157
Perceptions, 54
Perfect, 2, 130, 148
Person, 43, 55, 83, 90, 147–148, 154
Personal, 43, 45, 107, 142, 154
Perspective, 9, 12–13, 20, 41, 43, 46, 62–63, 72–73, 81, 83, 86, 93, 108–109, 120, 123, 136, 141, 148, 166
Persuasive, 12, 79
Pervade, 2, 48
Phenomenology, 8–9, 14, 20, 45, 58–59, 62, 105, 129, 135–136, 144, 163
Phenomenological, 39, 46–47, 55, 62, 83, 129
Philosophy, 1–2, 5, 8–9, 11–14, 16, 19–24, 27, 30, 39–42, 44–45, 47, 51, 54, 56, 58, 60, 62–64, 66, 71–73, 75–76, 78, 81–83, 85–86, 91–92, 94–95, 97–100, 103, 105–106, 109–111, 113, 117–118, 125, 129, 132–134, 137, 142–144, 163–168, 173–176, 179
Philosopher, 1–2, 8, 10, 12, 20, 27–28, 33, 36, 39, 43, 47, 53–54, 60, 64, 66, 71–75, 79, 82, 86, 90, 100, 107–108, 121, 130–132, 141, 144, 163–166, 171
Philosophical, 3, 8, 37, 44, 62, 73, 82, 109, 128, 132–133, 137, 141, 143, 165, 168, 175–176, 179
Pioneer, 2, 80, 132, 163, 174
Plato, 43, 90
Plumage, 131
Plume, 10

Poignant, 23
Pointers, 110
Poke, 108
Political, 121, 135, 143, 155
Portfolio, 118
Portion, 27, 79, 97, 128, 148, 179
Portrait, 111
Position, 10, 13, 15, 20, 27, 29–30, 41–42, 45, 56, 60, 65, 72–73, 76, 80, 84, 94, 100, 107, 119, 130–131, 142, 151, 171, 175
Possibility, 13, 24, 37–38, 61, 73, 106–107, 111, 133, 145, 175
Possible, 2, 17, 23, 25–26, 31, 33, 39, 45, 49, 56, 58, 61, 63–64, 67, 69, 80–81, 83, 90–91, 105, 108, 117–118, 121, 165–166, 173, 176
Postmortem, 9, 22, 36–37, 57, 69, 128
Posthumous, [also see: Works]
Postpone, 24
Postulation, 64, 132
Post-war, 110
Potential, 17, 39, 46, 64, 118
Power, 25, 121, 123, 143–144
Powerhouse, 71
Practical, 72, 135, 143, 145
Precedes, 100, 106, 123
Precedes ethics, 100
Precedes existence, 106
Precept, 164, 167–168
Precognition, 122
Preconceived, 31, 41, 44, 61, 168
Precondition, 99
Predetermined, 109
Preeminence, 113
Premature, 10, 86, 105
Pre-reflexive, 155

209

INDEX

Pressure, 136
Presumption, 13, 63, 73, 113, 118, 120, 132
Presumptuous, 72
Presupposition, 99, 164
Primordial, 119
Principle, 54–55, 64, 75, 112, 143, 157–158, 176
Priority, 47
Prism, 28, 46, 49, 100, 142, 174
Prolegomenon, 164
Prolific, 8, 14, 76, 96
Prominence, 79
Promise, 17, 24–25, 27, 29, 46, 56, 90
Promising, 27
Prophecy, 100
Propriety, 58, 175
Proscribe, 154
Protest, 98
Prowess, 39, 74, 179
Pseudo, 66
Pseudo-moral, 33, 47
Psychic, 145
Psychoanalysis, 25, 148, 168
Publication, 3, 5, 8–9, 13–15, 21, 23–25, 27, 29, 36, 38, 41–42, 44, 46, 48, 53–55, 57–59, 62, 64–65, 69, 71, 74–79, 82, 87, 89, 92, 96–97, 110, 118, 128–129, 146, 157, 164, 175, 177, 179
Publiés, [also see: Publish]
Publish, 27, 29, 36–37, 78, 96
Punchy, 131
Pursuit, 25, 46, 123
Puzzling, 149, 174
Qualitatively, 93
Quality, 14, 44, 79, 84, 86
Quantitative, 77
Quantitatively, 93
Quantity, 44, 86
Queries, 149

Questions, 2, 24–27, 38–39, 45, 148, 174
Quick, 23, 79, 90, 131
Quiddity, 125
Quote, 38, 46
Radical, 30
Raison, 37
Rambling, 8
Ramifications, 20, 67, 106, 109–111, 117, 132, 134, 161
Reacquaint, 176
Reaction, 119
Realistic, 54, 131, 141, 143–144
Reapprehended, 26
Rearranged, [also see: Works]
Reason, 2, 17, 22–24, 28–29, 35–36, 39, 41–42, 44, 46, 48, 51, 55–58, 63–64, 69, 76–79, 81, 84–85, 87, 89, 91–92, 94, 107, 112, 115, 117, 128, 132, 135, 155, 164–165, 173
Reasoning, 48–49, 77, 96, 129
Rebuff, 28, 42, 106
Rebuke, 14–15, 23, 28, 41–42, 71, 93, 105, 112, 167
Rebuking, 29
Rebuttal, 30, 108, 149
Receptive, 128
Reciprocal, 145
Recount, 12, 95, 125
Recurrent, 127
Reference, 12, 20, 41, 59, 80
Reflect, 13, 20, 42, 44, 55, 64, 93, 106, 109, 120, 132, 143, 161, 175
Reflecting, 155, 173
Reflection, 27, 108, 135
Refuse, 76, 100
Refusal, 79, 106, 108, 112
Refute, 11, 13–14, 28–30, 33, 41, 45, 48, 62–66,
74, 80, 84, 98, 106, 125, 131, 133, 146, 148–149, 165, 173
Refutation, 76, 100, 174
Reign, 26
Relation, 26, 85, 90, 100, 119, 142, 147–148, 156
Relational, 106
Relationship, 47, 58, 67, 107, 119, 122, 134, 137, 147, 151, 156
Relentless, 74
Reliable, 15, 105
Reluctant, 127
Reluctantly, 61
Remediate, 83
Renoncé, 37
Repertoire, 1, 77, 94, 97
Represent, 24, 38
Resist, [also see: John]
Resort, 148
Respect, 112
Responsible, 55
Responsibility, 26, 107, 110–112
Reste, 37
Reveal, 25, 49, 66, 81, 84, 86, 113, 122
Revelations, 72
Review, 8, 21, 23–24, 31, 51, 56–58, 107
Revolution, 67
Revolutionized, 163
Rhetoric, 79
Right, 14, 38–39, 42, 55–56, 71, 118, 134, 149, 156
Rightful, 61
Rigid, 30, 42
Rigidity, 154
Rigor, 90
Rigorous, 59
Roadmap, 63, 108–109
Rome, 94–98
Rudimentary, 81
Ruman Ji, [also see: Commentators]
Ruse, 148
Sample, 97

Satisfaction, 108
Scarcity, 15, 60
Schilpp Paul Arthur, 72, 86
Scholar, 1, 3, 9, 13–15, 23, 28–29, 48, 54, 59–60, 65, 74–75, 84, 86, 91–92, 94, 125, 128–129, 135–136, 145, 165, 179
Scholarly, 15, 23, 133
Schools of thought, 54
Science, 154
Search, 83, 108, 119, 149, 157
Secret, 36, 45
Self, 25, 99, 103, 111, 117, 121–122, 145, 147–148, 158
Self-activated, 146
Self-cause, 168
Self-conscious, 147
Self-determining, 146
Self-fulfilling prophecy, 100
Self-given duty, 74
Self-identity, 115, 121
Self-interest, 168
Sensible, 29
Sexual, 147
Shaky, 93
Shortsighted, 64, 77
Siècle, 180
Siege, 1, 23
Signature, 101
Significance, 47, 80
Significant, 75, 130, 139, 142, 144, 148, 156, 166
Simplistic, 15, 60, 81, 83–84
Simply, 13, 22, 36, 39, 41, 112
Single-minded, 174
Situate, 26
Situation, 26, 37–38, 85, 121–122, 147, 154, 168
Skeptical, 107, 117
Skepticism, 144
Skeptics, 60–61

Skillful, 40
Slander, 20
Social, 44, 55, 99, 120–122, 124, 133–134, 136, 143, 153–157
Socialism, 120
Societal, 120, 134
Society, 55, 66, 120, 123, 134–135, 137, 151, 154, 156, 158
Sophisticated, 22
Sophistication, 83
Speculations, 2, 29–30, 81, 100, 106, 147
Speculative, 72, 84, 91
Spontaneity, 146
Spontaneous, 25
Stand-alone, 62, 105, 168, 174
Stone Robert, 1, 3, 12–14, 16, 23, 74, 94–95, 101–102, 125, 128–129, 133–138, 151, 154–157, 159
Storm, 2, 113
Strategy, 64, 84
Structure, 10–12, 94, 135–136, 154
Struggle, 22, 115, 119, 154, 158
Stylistic, 11
Subjective, 22, 30, 43, 55, 110, 121–123, 174
Subjectivity, 99, 119–121, 123, 148, 156, 158
Subject-to-subject, 122
Subjugate, 148
Subscribe, 41, 91
Substantial, 43
Substantive, 23, 112
Subversive, 99
Successful, 41, 64, 165
Superficial, 77
Superficially, 20, 59
Superfluous, 42, 165
Supernatural, 47
Swift, 167
Symbolize, 64
Sympathy, 72
Sync, 11

Synergetic, 67
Synthesis, 135
Synthetic, 25
System, 30, 154
Systematic, 20–21, 30, 156
Systemizing, 155
Tableau, 91, 111
Tandem, 47, 62, 137, 142, 175
Task, 12, 21, 30, 40, 85
Technique, 15, 21, 56–57, 105, 168
Tendency, 86, 111
Tentacles, 54, 134
Terminology, 54, 84
Testimony, 8, 175
Theorem, 167
Theoretical, 8, 15, 30, 38, 42, 51, 56, 62–63, 65, 69, 75, 77, 80, 89, 129, 137, 145
Theory, 20, 38, 49, 78, 101, 120, 164–165, 168
Thesis, 10, 44, 64, 158, 171
Think, 14, 28, 80, 132
Thinker, 2, 19, 40, 43–44, 54, 66, 71–72, 78–79, 167
Tide, 39
Trademark, 105, 137
Tradition, 54–55
Traditional, 163
Traditionally, 22
Trajectory, 38
Transcend, 119, 154
Treaties, 3, 9, 13, 81
Treatises, 130
Treatment, 39, 92
Trivial, 12, 45, 76, 85
Truth, 76, 81, 91, 157
Typewritten, 98
Typewritten manuscript, 98
Typewritten pages, 98
Unanimous, 127, 133
Unanswered, 108
Unattainable, 120
Unavoidable, 147, 157

INDEX

Unbelievers, 109
Unbiassed, 15
Unbridgeable, 47
Uncalled for, 30
Uncanny, 58, 149
Uncertain, 74, 137
Unclear, 14, 75, 91, 145
Uncompleted, 13, 29, 35, 37–38, 60, 64, 167
Unconvinced, 13, 145
Uncover, 8, 19–20, 79, 94, 98, 135, 173
Underdeveloped, 35, 129
Underestimated, 91
Underpinnings, 62–63, 167
Undertaken, 2, 90
Undervalue, 142
Undisclosed, 96
Undisputable, 24, 35, 72
Unethical, 10
Unexplored, 75
Unfair, 17, 19–20
Unfiltered, 168
Unfinished, [also see: Works]
Unforgiving, 75, 90
Unfounded, 44
Unidirectional, 122
Uniformed, 15, 21
Uniformity, 54
Unimportant, 19
Unimpressive, 22
Unique, 25
Unison, 133
Universal, 53–54, 136
Universality, 54
Universally, 35, 55, 90
Universe, 168
University, 96–98, 101, 113, 129, 135, 176
Unjust, 62
Unknown, 58, 75
Unorganized, 92, 97
Unquestionable, 144
Unrealistic, 15
Unremitting, 39
Unsuitable, 14
Unwise, 111
Useless, 167

Utility, 13
Vague, 14, 22, 25–27, 45, 48, 60, 63, 72, 78–79, 81, 98, 108, 113, 122, 127, 131, 149, 154, 156–157
Valid, 109, 148
Valor, 13, 40, 43, 45, 85, 164
Valuable, 58, 81, 133
Value, [also see: Vague]
Values, 25, 46, 55, 67, 83, 103, 120–121, 142, 149, 156–157, 166, 168
Viability, 30
Vietnam, 98
  Vietnam war, 98
  American, 98
Vigorously, 22, 149
Virginia, 155
Virtue, 54–55, 155
Vis-à-vis, 73, 100, 103
Viva, 64
Vivaciousness, 137
Voices, 76, 133
  Voice, 43, 62
Volumes, 89
  Volume, 3, 61, 65, 134, 175
Voluptuous, 3
Voting, 155
  Vote, 155
Vulnerability, 123
Want, 2, 21, 73, 120–123, 149, 154, 168
War, [also see: Vietnam]
Warrant, 17, 29, 132
Wary, 45
Weaken, 72
Wealth, 130
We-as-object, 123
We-as-subject, 123
Well-needed, 150
Western philosophy, 163
West virginia, 155
Wisdom, 112
Workers, 154
Writer, 8, 20, 40, 45, 57, 61

Years, 2, 8, 16, 48, 82, 84, 141, 175, 179
Yield, 21, 44, 84
  Yield a better understanding, 84
Zeal, 165

ABOUT THE AUTHOR

BEN WOOD JOHNSON, Ph.D.

Dr. Johnson is a social observer, a philosopher, and a multidisciplinary scholar. He writes about law, legal theory, education, public policy, politics, race and crime, and ethics.

Dr. Johnson graduated from Penn State University and Villanova University. He holds a Doctorate in Educational Leadership, a Master's degree in Political Science, a Master's degree in Public Administration, and a Bachelor's degree in Criminal Justice.

Dr. Johnson worked in law enforcement. He attended John Jay College of Criminal Justice. Dr. Johnson is fluent in several languages, including French, Spanish, Portuguese, and Italian.

Dr. Johnson enjoys reading, poetry, painting, and music. You may contact Dr. Ben Wood Johnson by e-mail. You may also reach him via the postal services. For other means of communication, see the information listed below.

ABOUT THE AUTHOR

Mailing Address
Eduka Solutions
330 W. Main St #214
Middletown, PA 17057

Email
E-mail Address: tkpubhouse@gmail.com

Social Media
Find Dr. Ben Wood Johnson on the following media platforms.

Twitter: @benwoodpost
Facebook: @benwoodpost

You may find Dr. Ben Wood Johnson on other online platforms, including his official blog site at www.benwoodpost.org. You may visit his website at www.benwoodjohnson.com. If you would like to learn more about Dr. Johnson's works, you may find them on his official bookstore at www.benwoodjbooks.com.

Other Works

Selected works by Ben Wood Johnson

1. Racism: What is it?
2. Jean-Paul Sartre and Morality: A Legacy Under Attack
3. Sartre Lives On
4. Forced Out of Vietnam: A Policy Analysis of the Fall of Saigon
5. Natural Law: Morality and Obedience
6. Cogito Ergo Philosophus
7. Le Racisme et le Socialisme: La Discrimination Raciale dans un Milieu Capitaliste
8. International Law: The Rise of Russia as a Global Threat
9. Citizen Obedience: The Nature of Legal Obligation
10. Jean-Jacques Rousseau: A Collection of Short Essays
11. Être Noir : Quel Malheur !
12. L'homme et le Racisme: Être Responsable de vos Actions et Omissions

13. Pennsylvania Inspired Leadership: A Roadmap for American Educators
14. Adult Education in America: A Policy Assessment of Adult Learning
15. Striving to Survive: The Human Migration Story
16. Postcolonial Africa: Three Comparative Essays about the African State
17. Surviving the Coronavirus
18. Go Back Where You Came From

Find other works by Dr. Ben Wood Johnson on his blog.

MY EDUKA SOLUTIONS

www.benwoodpost.org

www.teskopublishing.com

www.ingramcontent.com/pod-product-compliance
Lightning Source LLC
Chambersburg PA
CBHW070422010526
44118CB00014B/1867